Praise for **The 60-Second Commute**

"For anyone with the heart of an entrepreneur, this book will give you all the practical information you need, as well as a dose of inspiration, to get your home-based company off the ground. For telecommuters and anyone else doing the home-office juggle, this is guaranteed to offer advice and encouragement you need to work from home . . . and do it well."

—TOM ASACKER
Author, *Sandbox Wisdom: Revolutionize Your Brand with the Genius of Childhood*

"A highly informative, entertaining guide to the pleasures and pitfalls of working from home. Don't be home without it!"

—CLEO COY
Former Director of Buying & Merchandising, Waldenbooks

"For people who want to create a 'no spin' lifestyle of self-reliance and independence, *The 60-Second Commute* provides the pathway. If time is money, you'll be taking this book to the bank."

—BILL O'REILLY
The O'Reilly Factor

"This is a great guide to working from home from two pros who do it well . . . and with a sense of humor and a dose of fun. This is also must-reading for anyone thinking about a commute to their spare bedroom or even dining room table. If you don't read this, you're hurting nobody but yourself."

—MIKE CELIZIC
Author and National Sports Columnist

"Balancing career and family is a tough nut to crack. These two authors really nail it."

—MARTI BENJAMIN SHIENER
Vice President of Programming for "Healthy Solutions with Mariette Hartley"

"This is terrific!! THE BEST HOME OFFICE GUIDE EVER."

—CHARLES SPICER
Executive Editor, St. Martin's Press, New York City

"I absolutely believe that all the information in this book is the result of first-hand experience. Thanks to these two smart, successful and savvy women."

—TONY DIIOIA
Chairman/CEO, Animagic Entertainment, Santa Barbara, CA

"What a find!!! I love this book and I need the information."

—JACQUELINE D. BYRD, ESQ.
Columnist and Attorney, Bowie, Maryland

"An excellent, well-written, easy to read primer and reference book not only for newcomers to the home business field but also for those already established. Wish I had this book before I embarked on a home business—it would have made life a lot easier."

—ALYCE FINELL
President, Finell Enterprises

THE
60-SECOND
COMMUTE

ISBN 0-13-047728-1

FINANCIAL TIMES

In an increasingly competitive world, it is quality
of thinking that gives an edge—an idea that opens new
doors, a technique that solves a problem, or an insight
that simply helps make sense of it all.

We work with leading authors in the various arenas
of business and finance to bring cutting-edge thinking
and best learning practice to a global market.

It is our goal to create world-class print publications
and electronic products that give readers
knowledge and understanding which can then be
applied, whether studying or at work.

To find out more about our business
products, you can visit us at www.ft-ph.com

THE 60-SECOND COMMUTE

A GUIDE TO YOUR 24/7 HOME OFFICE LIFE

Erica Orloff

Kathy Levinson, Ph.D.

FINANCIAL TIMES

An Imprint of PEARSON EDUCATION

Upper Saddle River, NJ • New York • London • San Francisco • Toronto • Sydney
Tokyo • Singapore • Hong Kong • Cape Town • Madrid
Paris • Milan • Munich • Amsterdam

www.ft-ph.com

Library of Congress Cataloging-in-Publication Data

A CIP catalog record for this book can be obtained from the Library of Congress.

Editorial/production supervision: *Patty Donovan*
Composition: *Pine Tree Composition*
Cover Design Director: *Jerry Votta*
Cover Design: *Talar A. Boorujy*
Interior Design: *Meg Van Arsdale*
Manufacturing buyer: *Maura Zaldivar*

VP, Executive Editor: *Tim Moore*
Editorial Assistant: *Allyson Kloss*
Development Editor: *Russ Hall*
Marketing Manager: *Bryan Gambrel*
Full-Service Production Manager: *Anne R. Garcia*

© 2003 Pearson Education, Inc.
Publishing as Financial Times Prentice Hall
Upper Saddle River, New Jersey 07458

Financial Times Prentice Hall books are widely used by corporations and government agencies for training, marketing, and resale.

For information regarding corporate and government bulk discounts please contact:
Corporate and Government Sales (800) 382-3419 or corpsales@pearsontechgroup.com

Printed in the United States of America

10 9 8 7 6 5 4 3 2 1

ISBN 0-13-047728-1

Pearson Education LTD.
Pearson Education Australia PTY, Limited
Pearson Education Singapore, Pte. Ltd.
Pearson Education North Asia Ltd.
Pearson Education Canada, Ltd.
Pearson Educación de Mexico, S.A. de C.V.
Pearson Education—Japan
Pearson Education Malaysia, Pte. Ltd.
Pearson Education, Upper Saddle River, New Jersey

FINANCIAL TIMES PRENTICE HALL BOOKS

For more information, please go to www.ft-ph.com

Dr. Judith M. Bardwick
  Seeking the Calm in the Storm: Managing Chaos in Your Business Life
Gerald R. Baron
  Now Is Too Late: Survival in an Era of Instant News
Thomas L. Barton, William G. Shenkir, and Paul L. Walker
  Making Enterprise Risk Management Pay Off:
  How Leading Companies Implement Risk Management
Michael Basch
  CustomerCulture: How FedEx and Other Great Companies Put
  the Customer First Every Day
J. Stewart Black and Hal B. Gregersen
  Leading Strategic Change: Breaking Through the Brain Barrier
Deirdre Breakenridge
  Cyberbranding: Brand Building in the Digital Economy
William C. Byham, Audrey B. Smith, and Matthew J. Paese
  Grow Your Own Leaders: How to Identify, Develop, and Retain
  Leadership Talent
Jonathan Cagan and Craig M. Vogel
  Creating Breakthrough Products: Innovation from Product Planning
  to Program Approval
Subir Chowdhury
  Organization 21C: Someday All Organizations Will Lead this Way
Subir Chowdhury
  The Talent Era: Achieving a High Return on Talent
Sherry Cooper
  Ride the Wave: Taking Control in a Turbulent Financial Age
James W. Cortada
  21st Century Business: Managing and Working in the New
  Digital Economy
James W. Cortada
  Making the Information Society: Experience, Consequences,
  and Possibilities
Aswath Damodaran
  The Dark Side of Valuation: Valuing Old Tech, New Tech, and New
  Economy Companies
Henry A. Davis and William W. Sihler
  Financial Turnarounds: Preserving Enterprise Value
Sarv Devaraj and Rajiv Kohli
  The IT Payoff: Measuring the Business Value
  of Information Technology Investments

D. Quinn Mills
  *Buy, Lie, and Sell High: How Investors Lost Out on Enron
  and the Internet Bubble*
Dale Neef
  E-procurement: From Strategy to Implementation
John R. Nofsinger
  *Investment Blunders (of the Rich and Famous)...And What You Can Learn
  from Them*
John R. Nofsinger
  *Investment Madness: How Psychology Affects Your Investing...And What
  to Do About It*
Erica Orloff and Kathy Levinson, Ph.D.
  The 60-Second Commute: A Guide to Your 24/7 Home Office Life
Tom Osenton
  *Customer Share Marketing: How the World's Great Marketers Unlock
  Profits from Customer Loyalty*
Richard W. Paul and Linda Elder
  *Critical Thinking: Tools for Taking Charge of Your Professional
  and Personal Life*
Matthew Serbin Pittinsky, Editor
  *The Wired Tower: Perspectives on the Impact of the Internet
  on Higher Education*
W. Alan Randolph and Barry Z. Posner
  *Checkered Flag Projects: 10 Rules for Creating and Managing Projects
  that Win, Second Edition*
Stephen P. Robbins
  The Truth About Managing People...And Nothing but the Truth
Fernando Robles, Françoise Simon, and Jerry Haar
  Winning Strategies for the New Latin Markets
Jeff Saperstein and Daniel Rouach
  *Creating Regional Wealth in the Innovation Economy: Models,
  Perspectives, and Best Practices*
Eric G. Stephan and Wayne R. Pace
  *Powerful Leadership: How to Unleash the Potential in Others and Simplify
  Your Own Life*
Jonathan Wight
  Saving Adam Smith: A Tale of Wealth, Transformation, and Virtue
Yoram J. Wind and Vijay Mahajan, with Robert Gunther
  Convergence Marketing: Strategies for Reaching the New Hybrid Consumer

To Jay Poynor, our wonderful agent, who put up with these two women, our home offices, and our combined total of two husbands, five children, one Grandma Weezie, three dogs, one rabbit, and fifteen birds (and four goldfish!).

CONTENTS

ACKNOWLEDGMENTS

The authors gratefully acknowledge the unflagging support of their agent, Jay Poynor of The Poynor Group. His enthusiasm for this project never wavered, and his marketing and PR insights were very valuable. On a personal note, he is just a one in a million guy.

From our first conversation with Tim Moore, Vice President of Prentice Hall/Financial Times, we knew we had a home. His support of this project has been terrific, and he has always innately understood that millions and millions of people out there are creating home offices, often to find precious spare moments of family time in this 24/7 climate.

We thank Russ Hall for his work coordinating the technical reviews. While a stickler for details, he did keep us on track. We especially thank Cleo Coy for not only her comments, but her support and positivism. We also thank Toddi Gutner of *Business Week* for her insights. In addition, we'd like to acknowledge the production staff at Prentice Hall, including Patty Donovan of Pine Tree Composition. Also, Gardi Wilks and Bryan Gambrel for their PR and marketing efforts.

On a personal level, Erica would like to thank Cleo Coy, Nancy Hines, Pam Morrell, and the people who are most impacted by having a home office front and center in the middle of that crazy house of ours: John, Alexa, Nicholas, and Isabella. As I say time and time again in this book, on my worst day—phone ringing non-stop, dogs barking, children fighting, school calling to say someone forgot her lunch, clients needing me *right now*, along with a hundred other deadlines—I only commuted 60 seconds. And the reverse is true. At the end of that day, I have 60 seconds to go to happy hour, and 60 seconds to hugs from the most important little people in the world. And John, there's no better personal assistant anywhere—plus you make better food than anyone else.

On a personal note, Kathy would like to thank those nearest and dearest—Marc, Peter, Aimee, and Weezie. Marc, your belief and support in me makes it all possible. For Peter and Aimee—I love having the time and flexibility in my schedule to be able to see you so often in school. I am proud when I see your craving for books and writing. I don't mind that you hide books under the covers. For my mother, Weezie, whose enthusiasm helped on those crazy days. I probably should thank our giant Tibetan Mastiff, Ming, for not eating my disk when he had the opportunity.

Kathy would like to thank the Buckley Country Day School, particularly Head Master Thomas Reid, Ann Reid, and librarian Patricia Russac for providing that little slice of heaven in the back of the library.

Kathy would also like to thank Joseph Salamo, CPA, for generously sharing his time and expertise during tax season to read and review our tax chapter.

INTRODUCTION

This book is about the American Dream, and more. It is about the dream that you have secretly held onto, waiting for the right opportunity. It is about making the decision to go down the other path—the one that is yours alone. It is about taking stock of all your education, training and experience and realizing that it's time to live your life—your way and on your terms.

In our professional careers, both of the authors of this book have been commuters on trains, subways, highways, and airplanes. We know about standing on train platforms in sub-zero temperatures, and wondering how a minute could take so unbelievably long. We have fought our way on to over-crowded subway cars in sweltering heat and felt way too close to the person next to us. We've sat in bumper-to-bumper traffic with the gas gauge near empty and with no way to call in late for work.

What makes us so special? Nothing at all. We work, run a household, and raise kids just like everybody else. There is one exception—we do it all from home. We're living our lives—on site. Gone are the crazy commute and long hours away from our loved ones, pets, and home. These days our commute takes all of 60 seconds, the time it takes to walk from one room into another. Do we still work hard? Sometimes it feels as if we've never worked harder. Would we trade it all in and head back into the office? No chance.

Change can be unnerving. Change means traveling down an unchartered course, destination unknown. Remaining where you are and doing what you have always done means that at least you know where you are and what you can expect—more of the same. But if you're holding this book in your hands, you are thinking about change. You're thinking about expanding your life out to all its proportions and exciting possibilities.

Here are the authors' two stories of giving up the rat race for a commute from bedroom to desk—in about 60 seconds flat.

About Erica

No one told me that if I became a writer and book editor that one day it would be a lucrative way to make money working from home. In fact, though it would take a team of wild horses to get me to reveal my age (and I'd lie anyway), back when I graduated from college, no one worked from home. You

xix

just never heard about it. There was no e-mail. Faxes were a modern new invention, but other than freelance artists or the struggling novelist, no one had a home office. We all accepted that the daily grind was part of work. The idea that someone could wake up, put on a pot of coffee in his or her apartment or house, and walk in a bathrobe over to a desk with all the latest technology, and actually earn a living at it, was crazy. Unheard of.

I took a job in the publishing world and worked in an office, under ugly lights, overheated in winter in New York, and under-air-conditioned in summer swelter. By the time I had my first child, an opportunity came along for me to write articles for a newspaper freelance—from home. Technology had changed. Get paid to write from home, *now we were talking*. This was something I could really get used to. I don't think I've ever looked back.

For me, it was always about my kids. I didn't need a corner office and a plaque on my door to tell me who I was. My family will tell you I was weird (I prefer eccentric) all along—even as a kid. Maybe it was only natural that once I figured out that a 60-second commute was a possibility, I jumped at the chance. I never could make it to the office at nine o'clock anyway. I was always the woman putting on her pantyhose in her car on the freeway, stuck in traffic. The one putting her mascara on using the rearview mirror. Yeah, that was me.

By my second child, I had a modest business going editing books and making about $50,000 a year. Not bad, considering I didn't have to wear pantyhose, and I also never had to miss a first step of my son or a school play of my daughter. As much as I was enjoying being home with my kids full-time, another thought crossed my mind: Even if I didn't have kids, if they magically were 18 tomorrow and flew the coop, I would never, ever, *ever* want to work in an office again. My freedom was too important to me.

By my third child, my modest business had tripled. Not only was I commuting in my jeans and a T-shirt, I was making more money than many of the people taking the train to work, rising at dawn just to make it to their desks at nine o'clock. And wherever I went—cocktail parties, doctors' offices, the park—if people asked what I did, and I said I was a writer and editor and worked from home, men and women alike would become fascinated. This 60-second commute, as scary, exhilarating, and chaotic as it might be at times, was something many people apparently wanted to do. They asked questions. A lot of questions. So many questions that I realized I would need a book to explain it all. How to do it, well and happily, how to juggle, how to deal with taxes and lawyers, and incoming calls when the dog is barking and you can't concentrate. All the nitty-gritty about working from home. Including getting to your desk in 60 seconds—on a slow day.

About Kathy

I went to school for a long time and accumulated quite a few degrees. After years of clinical work as a school psychologist, family therapist, and clinical supervisor, I opened my own practice. It was my life's dream—or so I thought. I found a charming office and threw a grand-opening party. But in spite of the beautiful and cozy office with piped-in music and my own coffee pot, I was isolated and bored. At the end of the day I felt drained and empty. I kept hearing singer Peggy Lee in my head, "Is that all there is?"

I always imagined that later in my career I would work from home and write. I had this idea that working from home was for those who were winding down from a stellar career, certainly not starting one. That point of view was flipped on its head with one single phone call. In just seven days, my husband and I would become the parents of a six-month-old boy from Vietnam. There wasn't even a diaper no less a crib in our home. The arrival of my son was a defining moment in my life. I knew at that moment exactly what I wanted. I wanted to work from home and raise my son.

I left private practice and opened a small publishing company from my house. A lot of people shook their heads and thought I was nuts. They believed I was tossing all those clinical years out the window. That's not how I saw it. I saw it as a fantastic opportunity to take my training and experience and turn it into something that was tailor-made to suit my life. I was still a psychologist—that hadn't changed. I was dying in that private practice, but now I felt liberated.

The road into publishing was filled with wild highs and nail-biting lows. One of the first books I published was my own, *First Aid for Tantrums*. When the media noticed the book, the phone started ringing. I was flown to New York to appear on *Good Morning America* and *MSNBC*. I went nose-to-nose with the feisty Bill O'Reilly who admitted on television that he drove all those nuns crazy back in parochial school. I survived Sally Jesse Raphael's raucous audience and was invited back two more times. I crossed the country doing a weeklong national book tour, being escorted from television studio to radio station to newspaper reporter. It was a thrill to meet new people in all these cities.

The work was hard and the deadlines were stressful but I loved publishing from a home office. There are moments I will never forget—like the time my son danced naked on the front lawn while I was doing a live radio interview or the day when I first saw my book printed in another language.

As high as I soared as an author, I struggled as a publisher. My small publishing company just couldn't compete against the giants. The failure nearly shattered my confidence to say nothing of the gaping whole it put in my family's bank account. It was not an easy time.

Everybody loves 20/20 hindsight. When I look back, I can see where the mistakes were made. Some were caused by a national distributor whose business ethics were less than honorable. My accountant and lawyer urged me to pursue legal avenues, but the till was empty. The other mistakes were mine. I entered publishing with little experience and without a business plan. I thought I was bright enough to figure it all out. These are classic mistakes for anyone starting a new business.

Bruised and beaten—you bet. Then why didn't I tattoo a big "L" on my head for loser? The way I see it in life there are choices to make: You can either move forward when you stumble or hide under the bed. I made a decision to be a small publisher and it didn't work out. People fail every day. I made the decision to move on.

How did I succeed if I failed? I succeeded because during my years as a small publisher, I learned every aspect of the business from developmental editing to designing book covers. Sure, I learned the hard way, but I did learn. I found out that there were aspects of publishing that I was pretty good at, such as writing and appearing on television. I took those skills and freelanced myself out to other publishers—all from my home office. The best part is that I haven't missed a minute with my children, and I am writing my own books again.

Today, I am not only a psychologist but also an author and a public speaker. My home office gives me the freedom to raise my children, run my household, care for my mom who now lives with us, and boost my family's income. I like how that success feels to me.

About the 60-Second Commute

The 60-Second Commute is your guide to setting up and beginning your home office. It is designed to provide ideas, answer questions, and offer guidance and information every step of the way. Whether you are a telecommuter, moonlighter, consultant, or business owner, there is something in this book for you. The book is based on the combined twenty-two years of experience from authors Erica Orloff and Kathy Levinson, Ph.D.

How This Book is Laid Out

The 60-Second Commute consists of 15 chapters, 4 appendices, and a glossary. Each chapter is filled with practical and useful information that will show you how to get started in a home office. From setting up your home office to finding childcare and filing your taxes, you'll find that this book has left no stone unturned.

- **Chapter 1: Next Stop—Home**
  Did you know that nearly 60 million people work from a home office at least one day a week? There's a buzz out there, and it's making its way across the country—work from home, pursue your passion, and take hold of your life. Find out who started at their kitchen table and are enjoying amazing success today. Take our quiz and learn if working from home is for you. Discover why those who work from a home office have no plans to commute ever again.

- **Chapter 2: Creating Space for Your 60-Second Commute**
  Creating space for your home office is an essential first step. Whether your home is a cottage, apartment, boat, or a house, you will need to create a space to work. In this chapter, we discuss how to set up your work space in a way that works best for you.

- **Chapter 3: Technology: 60-Second Commute Essentials**
  All home office professionals need equipment. This chapter covers it all, from computers to fax machines, and provides reader-friendly descriptions of such topics as DSL lines, cable modems, and ISDN. If you're not sure what you need in your home office or how to set it all up, this chapter will answer your questions.

- **Chapter 4: The 24/7 Lifestyle: Time Management in the Home Office**
  Time, the one thing we all seem to need more of but aren't sure how to get it. This chapter describes how to maximize your time, avoid interruptions, and improve your overall productivity.

- **Chapter 5: Organization: How to Get Your Act Together**
  Nothing can foul up a dream faster than disorganization. The chapter starts off with confessions of two disorganized women and describes some of the pitiful mistakes Erica and Kathy have made along the way. It's followed by a quiz to see how organized you really are. Next you'll find a step-by-step guide for getting organized, as well as tips for managing the invasions of those little people in your home.

- **Chapter 6: Professionalism in the Home Office**
  This chapter will help you to put your best professional face on while working from a home office. Whether you are telecommuter or a small business owner, you don't want to lose credibility by appearing less than professional. This chapter covers stationary and business cards, brochures, telephone systems, and constructing eye-catching websites.

- **Chapter 7: Get the Ball Rolling: Business & Budget Plans**
  Once you make the decision to start a home business, it is time to roll up your sleeves and tend to the business of planning and becoming legitimate. This chapter provides a detailed description of legal structures and business plans. We will discuss how to name and register your business name, incorporate your business, register a website, and determine your start-up costs. There is a detailed checklist and worksheet designed to get you on your way to success.

- **Chapter 8: Taxes: Don't Get Caught Asleep at the Wheel**
  We take the fear out of taxes by providing a step-by-step guide of what you need to know about taxes, from how to pick your accountant to the latest in software programs. This chapter covers accounting methods, home office deductions, quarterly taxes, and how you can fly below the IRS's radar and stay clear of trouble.

- **Chapter 9: Legal Eagles: Understanding Your Business and the Law**
  Beginning a business from home is exciting and for many, a life long dream. Learn how to establish your business correctly from the start so that you can reap the rewards later on. This chapter covers how to hire a lawyer, apply for licenses and permits, apply for patents and copyrights, and protect your trade secrets.

- **Chapter 10: Insurance in the Home Office**
  If you are starting your own business, you may want health insurance and life insurance. This chapter describes your health insurance options, COBRA, as well as other insurance options. Learn how to make wise insurance decisions and where to go for more information.

- **Chapter 11: Pink Slip Blues**
  You had a hunch that it could happen to you—and then it did. Being handed your pink slip and losing your job can be a frightening and unsettling experience. Learn what steps to take before you lose your job and what to do if you are laid off. Find out how to start over, avoid scams, and pursue what you really want to do.

- **Chapter 12: Child Care: Life on the High Wire**
  Child care is an essential part of the home office pie. In this chapter, we discuss the many choices available, from babysitters to au pairs, and how to pick the right person to look after your children.

- **Chapter 13: Strategies for Hanging in When the Going Gets Tough**

  Business, as in life, has its highs and lows. There are days, even months, when nothing seems to be going well. In this chapter, we discuss how to recharge your batteries when you're feeling rundown and beat those occasional feelings of isolation. Find out about the top-ten things you can do when your business is in danger of failing and how you can turn it around.

- **Chapter 14: Telecommuting Proposals: Getting into the Home Office**

  More and more companies are offering telecommuting programs to their employees. Often the decision of who gets to work from home is left up to managers. If you would like your boss to give you a 60-second commute, turn to this chapter to find out how to write a telecommuter proposal.

- **Chapter 15: Marketing Yourself and Your Small Business**

  Whether you are a telecommuter who needs to network your contacts or a business owner who needs to get off the ground, you'll need to market yourself. This chapter is full of networking and marketing ideas that teach you how to seize opportunities, think outside the box, and go outside your comfort zone.

Appendices

At the back of *The 60-Second Commute*, we include four appendices filled with contact and website information for government resources, organizations, associations, start-up assistance, and best websites.

- **Appendix A—Government Resources:** In this appendix, you will find contact information for the Internal Revenue Service (IRS), the Small Business Administration (SBA), the Copyright Office, and more.

- **Appendix B—Organizations and Associations:** In this appendix, you will find contact information for many of the useful organizations and associations that provide helpful information, newsletters, online resources, expert guidance, products and services.

- **Appendix C—Start-up Assistance:** There are many resources available to help you on your way to successfully running a home office.

This appendix will provide you with contact and website information regarding office supplies, sample business plans and forms, and more.

- **Appendix D—Web Hot Spots:** This appendix lists some of the valuable websites we have discovered while doing research for *The 60-Second Commute*.

CHAPTER 1

Next Stop—Home

Every day, 60 million (yes, million) people are getting out of bed, walking in their bathrobe with a cup of coffee to a desk somewhere in their home or apartment, and working from home. They have a 60-second commute. One minute. No subway, no obnoxious guy or gal in the next cubicle, just freedom. In the era of faxes and e-mail, it has become a new American dream. Is it a passing fad? Not according to builders who predict that in the next 5 years, almost all new homes will have dedicated home offices sketched into the blueprints. There's a buzz out there, and it's making its way across the country—work from home, pursue what you love, and take hold of your own life. Want to join them but not sure if you're ready? Here's a little surprise for you—you are already on your way.

A person makes the decision to work from home for a lot of different reasons. For some people, the decision is like a loud gong sounding in their heads, "That's it! I've had it. I can be just as productive and a lot more comfortable at home." For them, the 6:47 A.M. commute on the train in the rain, snow, sleet, and hail has lost its zing. Or perhaps sitting snarled in traffic for the billionth time no longer holds the same magic. For others, it's about taking a risk and going for a life-long dream even if your family thinks you've flipped. Some people wish to spend more time with their kids. They figured out how to work and still be able to get the kids to

Why People Decide to Work From Home

- *Tired of being a road warrior*
- *Desire to be their own boss*
- *Want to escape from the corporate world and the doldrums of middle management*
- *Have been "Enron'ed"*
- *Feel restless, underappreciated, and underpaid*
- *Caught by the dot.com layoffs or corporate downsizing*
- *Pushed out by age*
- *Wish to be at home raising children*
- *Yearn for flexible hours*
- *Want to supplement their incomes*

music lessons, soccer, or Karate. They understand that time moves extraordinarily fast, and in the blink of an eye, children are grown and asking for your car keys. Others realize that working from home, whether it's starting a small business, consulting, telecommuting, or freelancing, is a wonderful way to boost their income. For them, the additional income helps pay for retirement, mortgages, vacations, school tuitions, or perhaps a little cosmetic surgery. The bottom line is that we are all motivated by different interests.

60 Seconds with Neil Smith

Neil Smith is the founder of a unique consulting firm, EHS Partners. With 19 professionals in 14 cities, it truly is a cutting-edge company. Smith's company consults with major corporations to dramatically increase their earnings. His philosophy is simple, "We must do one thing and one thing only—and be the best at it." Smith attracted the best professionals with the lure of working from home and by not having to relocate. Today, EHS Partners may be one of the largest "virtual" companies with revenues in excess of $30 million.

The greatest numbers of telecommuters can be found in industries that handle information, such as high-tech industries, banking, publishing, insurance, marketing, public relations (PR), advertising, consulting agencies, and some state and federal agencies. For an in-depth listing of companies with telecommuting programs, we recommend you visit the website Work-At-Home-Success at *www.workathomesuccess.com*.

Advances in technology, especially computers, faxes, and modern telephone systems with capabilities like teleconferencing (something we used while writing this book!), make working from home a bonus for telecommuters and a real opportunity for entrepreneurs and small business owners. Today's technology is so user-friendly, affordable, and portable that you can work from virtually anywhere—traveling on an airplane, vacationing, or watching your son's ice skating practice.

The numbers of those who are taking the leap and working from home is growing at a very fast rate. In fact, the federal government estimates that in 2002, 60 percent of Americans will spend some part of their

Name Calling

Ask a person who works from home what he or she does and they might use any of the following titles:

- *Freelancer*
- *Consultant*
- *Entrepreneur*
- *Self-employed*
- *Mompreneur*
- *Dadpreneur*
- *Small business owner*
- *Home-based businessperson*
- *Independent contractor*
- *Telecommuter*
- *Teleworker*
- *Moonlighter*
- *Open-collar worker*

workweek at home. That means that more than half the working population works from a home office (even if that's just their kitchen table). The International Telework Association and Council's annual survey shows that the number of employees who telework in the United States increased to 28.8 million, a jump of nearly 17 percent in just 1 year.

There is no question about it—women are rocking the home-based business world, making up one of the fastest-growing groups in the home office market. Perhaps out of a desire to be in charge of their own careers or a need to figure out a better way to earn a living and raise children, women are pushing the possibilities further every day. According to data from the U.S. Census Bureau and the National Foundation for Women Business Owners, there are over 3.5 million home-based, women-owned businesses in the United States. What is more, these businesses provide full- or part-time jobs to over 14 million people.

Home-based businesses have become viable professional options. Corporate downsizing and dot.com layoffs have prompted men and women to think outside the box and pursue alternative ways of earning a living. According to the American Home Business Association, 8,000 people start a home business

While a homemaker raising children, Lillian Vernon started a gift and home furnishing home business from the kitchen table in 1951. Today, Lillian Vernon's mail order catalog empire grosses over $241 million annually.

every day—that's 1 every 11 seconds. Today, estimates show that over 40 percent of the workforce in the United States operates from home. A large percentage are the entrepreneurs who have decided to take a chance and begin something all their own. The Kauffman Center for Entrepreneurial Leadership estimates that about 2 million one-person new businesses are started each year. There are about 33 million entrepreneurs working by themselves from home.

Big Dreams, Big Successes

The following is a list of individuals, some you may certainly recognize, who started out with a few dollars, a big dream, and a burning desire to blaze their own trails:

- **Michael Dell:** At the age of 12, Michael Dell was already an entrepreneur selling thousands of dollars of mail order stamps from his parents' home. As a senior in high school, Dell made $18,000 selling newspaper subscriptions to newlyweds. Against his parents' wishes, he dropped out of college at 19 to sell computers. Now in his 30s, Michael Dell is a billionaire and his company, Dell Computers, is a top *Fortune 500* company with sales in excess of $31 billion dollars.

- **Martha Stewart:** Martha Stewart's love for cooking and entertaining was so strong that while living in a 19th century farmhouse in the upscale bedroom community of Westport, Connecticut, she started a catering business. Her life has been in fast forward ever since. On October 19, 1999, Martha Stewart took her company public and became a billionaire. The Martha Stewart Living Omnimedia, Inc. empire includes 4 magazines; over 50 books on cooking, entertaining, crafts, and decorating; a cable television show; a syndicated column; a radio show; an Internet site; mail order catalogs; and over $763 million in annual sales for home decorating and furnishings. Though she has recently taken a beating in the public eye, Martha seems to be a survivor.

- **Jeff Bezos:** In 1994, Jeff Bezos quit a successful career and jumped into his Chevy Blazer with his wife and dog. Bezos wasn't exactly sure where he was going but figured he would know when he got there. Bezos believed that selling products on the Internet could be very successful and kept a list of products he wanted to sell online. When the couple landed in Seattle, Washington, they decided to stay. They rented a tiny house, and with very little money to spare, converted the garage into a warehouse for books. Today, Amazon.com is the world's largest bookstore. Bezos, now worth over $10 billion dollars, has been coined the "king of cybercommerce."

- **Margaret Rudkin:** In 1937, Margaret Rudkin began baking and selling a variety of fresh breads from her home. Thirty years later, her little bread business, better known as Pepperidge Farms, was enjoying sales in excess of $32 million when she sold it to the Campbell Soup Company.

- **Ruth and Elliot Handler:** Ruth and Elliot Handler, along with partner Harold Matson, created a picture frame company in a garage. When the partnership ended, the Handlers decided to make doll furniture and toys and called their company Mattel Toys. Ruth had a vision for a doll, but no one in the marketing department took her very seriously. Three years later, the doll named after her daughter, Barbie, was the talk of the 1959 New York Annual Toy Fair. Over 40 years later, Barbie is enjoying more success than ever. It's been said that if placed head to toe, Barbie dolls could wrap around the earth seven times.

- **Bill Hewlett and David Packard:** Bill and David's excellent adventure began in 1938 in Packard's garage in Palo Alto, California. Hewlett and Packard were classmates at Stanford when a professor convinced them to start an electronics company. With barely $500 between them, the two friends rolled up their sleeves and got started. In 1972, their hand-held calculator called the HP-35 was a wild success and marked the beginning of the personal computing industry. Today, the Hewlett-Packard corporation earns over $47 billion a year. The garage where it all started is now a registered historical landmark and reads, "The birthplace of Silicon Valley."

- **Hugh Hefner:** In his silk pajamas and slippers, Hugh Hefner has to be the quintessential home office entrepreneur. As the founder and publisher of *Playboy* magazine, Hefner has been working from home for nearly 50 years. Hefner's dream was to create a mainstream men's magazine that included talk and photos of nude women. The course of Hefner's life changed forever when he acquired photographs of the young Marilyn Monroe in the nude. With the photos in hand and a loan from his mother, Hefner launched *Playboy* magazine. Hefner did the first layout of the magazine at his kitchen table. The first issue quickly sold out, and Hefner's empire was born. He broke new ground by weaving his sophisticated and relaxed view of sexuality into the pages of his magazine. Hefner didn't want to just talk about the *Playboy* lifestyle, he wanted to live it. In 1971, the company went public on the stock exchange. The magazine was selling at a rate of over 7 million copies a month. Hefner expanded the *Playboy* name beyond the magazine by opening 23 adult clubs where beautiful women in provocative "bunny" outfits served drinks; producing a television show, adult movies, books; and licensing the *Playboy* name. Today at age 77, Hugh Hefner is still working and partying from the *Playboy* mansion and living life—his way.

Another population not to overlook are the baby boomers who are growing older—albeit grudgingly. Americans who were born between 1946 and 1964 are 76 million strong and represent the largest single sustained growth of the population in the history of the United States. For this group, 50 is definitely not old. Many baby boomers would say that they're just getting started. The fact is, we are living longer—and living well. Travel through the Sun Belt states—Florida, Arizona, Nevada, New Mexico, and Texas—

Life expectancies are increasing in the United States. In 2000, the over-65 population grew to 34.9 million. In the first decade of the 21st century the over-65 population will grow another 10 to 12 percent—but between 2010 and 2030, the projected increases jump to 31.2 percent and 25.6 percent as the baby boom generation finally becomes senior citizens. In the year 2030, 21 percent of the population, or 65 million Americans, will be 65 years or older (World Almanac, 2001, p. 368).

and you'll discover legions of seniors well into their 70s, 80s, and even 90s who are living full, meaningful lives. Not only are they playing golf and tennis, but they're working. A growing number hold part-time jobs, freelance, act as consultants, or develop small businesses right from their home. Use the word elderly around this crowd and you could get hurt.

The American Association of Retired Persons (AARP) reports that baby boomers have put an interesting spin on retirement. Traditionally, the transition into retirement meant long leisurely days filled with reading, puttering around the house, and afternoon naps. Many baby boomers—8 in 10— say that they plan to continue working after they retire, at least on a part-time basis. One reason is because we're all living longer, healthier lives. Some see retirement as the beginning to the second half of their lives. Trends suggest that baby boomers are starting new careers, going back to college, creating niche businesses, and living their dreams, such as opening up bed and breakfast inns.

The other reason baby boomers plan to keep working after retirement is economics. Living longer means that your retirement dollars have to stretch further to ensure you don't outlive your savings. Currently over 65,000 people 100 years and over live in this country. So ask yourself this question: Do I have enough to live on if I should live to be 100?

No question about it, there are rewards and drawbacks to working from home. While the benefits include a 60-second commute to your home office, more control over your life, and freedom from the corporate world, it also calls for equal parts of discipline, organization, and flexibility. Unlike the office, there's no boss hovering over your shoulder checking to see what you're doing. Because you are the king or queen of your own domain and can make your own hours, there's always the temptation to put things off until later. Additionally, when you work from a home office, you're never really away from work because it's always there—in the other room. Running a household, balancing family life, and defending yourself from countless interruptions can be enough to push you over the waterfall (on some days).

Do You Have Enough to Retire?

To begin with, you'll need 70 percent of your annual preretirement income to maintain your current lifestyle during retirement.

- *Step 1: Calculate the amount equal to at least 70 percent of your income.*
- *Step 2: Figure out if your retirement plan—Social Security benefits, savings, 401(k)s, and other pension plans—will generate enough income.*

How do these calculations figure up to the plans you're making? Will you have enough?

The Downside of Not Working at the Office

1. No impromptu chats and meetings with colleagues means less feedback

2. Not being able to escape from work

3. Being interrupted by family and friends

4. Having work interfere with family relationships

5. Feeling overlooked by management back at the office—"Out of the loop"

6. Fear that working from home will hurt chances for career advancement

7. Feelings of isolation and loneliness

8. A tendency to overwork to prove your worthiness at the office

9. Trying to sound "professional" with background noise and perhaps children's sounds and commotion when on the phone

10. Sometimes it feels as if your day is never going to end

The Upside to Working From Home

1. No more hectic commutes

2. No boss breathing down your neck if you're a few minutes late

3. Less need for suits, dresses, ties, high heels, or pantyhose

4. When your child is sick, you don't have to ask permission to stay home

5. You can attend events at your child's school—even be class parent

6. You are more available for your children

7. Advances in technology link you to business without having to leave the comfort of your home (or your pajamas)

8. You can plan your work schedule around your life

9. No more office politics and power struggles

10. You have the potential for making more money

Is Working on Your Own Right for You?

If working from home is something you would like to try, then knowing what your strengths and weaknesses are can set you on a smooth course. Some of the answers to this quiz may seem obvious to you. After all, you're an intelligent person and you know what you should or shouldn't do. You probably know that it is important to be organized, but are you? You probably know that procrastinating is a bad thing, but do you? Try to answer the questions according to the way you manage your life right now. Be honest. This is your life we're talking about. If you want to be successful, you have to be your own best coach. If you really have a dream of working from home or even starting your own business, it is important to know if you are ready.

The idea behind this quiz is not that there is a certain type of person who can be successful working from home while another cannot. In reality, people who work from home come in all shapes and variations. But those who are the most successful at working from home seem to share common characteristics. Perhaps you don't possess those traits. Does that mean you should give up your plan or your dream? Certainly not. It does mean that there are areas you might want to tune up before you take the plunge into working from home. Knowing what those areas are, whether they are procrastination or confidence, is half the battle. You have to know what it is that needs changing in order to make the change.

After you finish the quiz, tally up your answers. If you find that you're well equipped to work from home then don't waste a second getting started. If you realize that there are areas to work on, then perhaps you should attend to them before you take the plunge.

Choose the statement that best answers the questions below.

1. When I am working on a job:
   a. I need total silence to concentrate.
   b. I prefer soft music to get me in the zone.
   c. Noise and interruptions don't bother me much.
2. When it comes to starting a new job:
   a. I like having a supervisor around in case I get hung up.
   b. I like to know exactly what my job description is.
   c. I like the challenge of having to figure it out on my own.

3. When it comes to working long hours:
   a. Long hours wear me down.
   b. I prefer to keep to my agreed-upon contractual hours.
   c. Hard work invigorates me.

4. When it comes to preparing my taxes:
   a. I'm usually rummaging through file boxes at midnight on April 14th.
   b. I try to improve my preparation style each year.
   c. I have a system that keeps me organized and ready all year.

5. When the mail arrives each day:
   a. I toss it onto the kitchen counter and move it when it threatens to take over the kitchen.
   b. I go through it every couple of weeks.
   c. I sort, toss, and file as it comes in.

6. When it comes to paying bills:
   a. I pay what I can afford and put the rest in a pile.
   b. I leave one day in my day planner for paying bills and filing.
   c. I pay my bills on the 15th and 30th of each month.

7. Some people make a To-Do List but:
   a. What's a To-Do List?
   b. I keep an ongoing list in my head.
   c. I keep a steno pad with my lists in the car next to me.

8. When it comes to career paths, I believe:
   a. You should stick with what you were trained to do even if it's not what you expected.
   b. You should consult with others to see if you should change careers.
   c. You should do what makes you feel happy and alive.

9. When I see everyone going in a certain direction, I tend to:
   a. Get worried and feel unsure what to do.
   b. Figure that the crowd must know something I don't so I join along.
   c. Follow the path that makes the most sense to me.

10. When I work with others, I prefer:
    a. I don't like working with anyone.
    b. To be a team player and let the group make decisions.
    c. To take a leadership position.

11. When I receive phone calls, my style is to:
    a. Call back if it's important to me.
    b. Add the call to the list of people I need to call back.
    c. Call back quickly, usually within a few hours.

12. When my work schedule gets interrupted:
    a. I usually take it out on everyone around me.
    b. I get agitated and have trouble settling back down.
    c. I go with it, and figure out another way to get my work done.

13. When it comes to following a set routine, I find that:
    a. I feel calmer knowing what my day is going to look like.
    b. Routines bore me.
    c. Routines keep me on track, but I'm never surprised by the unexpected.

14. When life gets chaotic:
    a. I stay put and wait for the dust to settle.
    b. I wonder if I am doing the right thing.
    c. I take a deep breath and keep walking forward.

15. When it comes to multitasking:
    a. I find that I never get to finish any of the tasks.
    b. I prefer taking on one thing at a time.
    c. I welcome the challenge.

16. When it comes to risk-taking:
    a. I like to play it fast and loose.
    b. I figure I have a 50/50 chance of making it.
    c. I bet on myself and not the odds.

17. When it comes to analyzing the facts and making decisions:
    a. I prefer to have a consultation with my astrologer.
    b. With all my degrees I'm bound to make a good decision.
    c. I rely on my instincts and my own street smarts.

18. When it comes to this business idea:
    a. All businesses are basically the same.
    b. It's what I've been doing for years.
    c. I'm brand-new to it, but I plan on making a business plan first.
19. When it comes to a financial strategy:
    a. When the money starts coming in, finances won't be an issue.
    b. I have some savings and credit cards.
    c. I've got money set aside in case I need it.
20. When problems arise:
    a. I figure that somebody let me down.
    b. I tend to let the answering machine screen out my calls.
    c. I don't make excuses.
21. I've made the decision to try this business venture because:
    a. I've heard of quite a few people who have made big money on this.
    b. I've always wanted to have my own business.
    c. I've done my homework, and I'm prepared to give this a try.
22. When it comes to legal and accounting matters:
    a. Those do-it-yourself guides are as good as anyone else.
    b. I plan on hiring a good accountant and lawyer, but I have to make some money first.
    c. I plan on using professionals with solid reputations from the be-ginning.
23. When I look at other people who have failed:
    a. I assume that they're just inexperienced.
    b. Statistically, some people are just not going to make it.
    c. I take a closer look to see if I can avoid some of the problems they faced.
24. When it comes to keeping deadlines:
    a. I take deadlines with a grain of salt and figure that people need to be flexible.
    b. I often wait until the last minute because I work best under pressure.
    c. When I make a deadline, I keep it.

25. When it comes to creating a budget plan:

   a. Business plans are for large companies with employees and overhead.

   b. I did look at a few sample budget plans.

   c. Business plans are like maps and are meant to keep you on course.

Determine Your Score

Your score on this quiz can range from 0 to 75. Remember to use your score as an indicator of strengths and weaknesses. This is hardly a personality test.

For each question you answered with an A, score 0; score 2 points for each B; and give yourself 3 points for each C.

70 – 75	You have excellent skills and a natural ability to be successful working from home. Now get going!
45 – 70	Well done. You have many of the qualities necessary to be successful in a home office. Improve your strengths, do your homework, and plan carefully.
Below 45	Put the brakes on for a while and take the time to get more experience. Your excitement to work from home may be greater than your ability to handle it. Seek out a few people who are successful working from home and study them closely.

Do You Have the Right Stuff?

How did you do on that quiz? If you didn't score as well as you would have liked, don't be disheartened. In fact, consider your low score a good thing because it means you were honest and you now know your strengths and weaknesses. Try not to be fooled into thinking that the right stuff is something you are born with, or that it's some obscure quality others have but you do not. Success starts with a dream and a plan. Listed below are some of the characteristics that many people who work from home report as helpful in their success.

Flexibility: Flexibility is essential if you have any dreams (or hopes) of working from home. Between the telephone, e-mails, front door, mail carrier, your family, and the dog, interruptions are a constant. On the other hand, situations in your business may come up that demand you take a different course or make a last-minute decision.

Multitasking: A multitasker is someone who can do many things at the same time. When you work from home, the ability to be a multitasker is key to your survival—and your sanity. You can pick up where you left off without losing momentum or flow.

Judgment: You just can't put a price tag on good judgment, no matter how smart you think you are or how many degrees you've accumulated. Judgment means that you can look at the whole picture and sort through the details to make sound decisions. Some would call it the ability to think on your feet.

Tenacity: Business, just as life, never goes smoothly all the time. There are ups and downs, disappointments, and uncertainty. Tenacity means that you can seatbelt yourself in and ride through the tough times.

Discipline: When you work from home, whether it's as a telecommuter, a consultant, or a small business owner, there is no one looking over your shoulder making sure that you're working. You are your own boss. Procrastination can hide around every corner.

Organization: The importance of being organized cannot be overemphasized. It's so important that we have devoted a whole chapter to it in this book.

Get on Board

Working from your home office may give you the things you have been longing for—more time with your family, work that you're passionate about, and the freedom to be your own boss. As in life, before making any decision it's wise to consider the pros and cons. Jumping blindly into a situation you are not prepared for will almost certainly lead to problems and disappointment. If working from home is something you would like to do, then don't let the challenges scare you. Come on, there are challenges around every corner—that's what life is all about. There are challenges in the corporate world—commuting, office politics, deadlines, and pink slips. There are challenges in relationships, parenthood, being a homeowner—you name it. Heck, there are challenges just trying to get through the supermarket. Now ask yourself this question: Wouldn't you rather reach for a dream then never have tried at all?

CHAPTER 2

CREATING A SPACE FOR YOUR 60-SECOND COMMUTE

If you want to set up a home office, there's one key element you need before you get rolling—a home! Whether it's an apartment, cottage, condominium, cabin in the woods, mansion, ranch house, or Cape Cod charmer, if you work from home, you will need to create a space from which to work inside that home.

This may sound simple enough, but in fact, creating a professional space that can co-exist with your nonprofessional life, as well as, often, gremlins (a.k.a. those cute kids you have), can require careful planning and thought.

A Room with a View—of the Laundry

Let's start with the physical office. First, it would be nice if you had an actual dedicated office with a door. Note we said it would be *nice*. Isn't it funny how *reality* creeps into these plans and dreams? A dedicated office isn't always possible. People have home offices on their dining room or kitchen tables or in their bedrooms. We even know someone who worked from his spacious walk-in closet—he had conference calls among his suits and ties.

If shortage of space is an issue, read up on our organization chapter, because it becomes especially important to keep clutter to a minimum. Add children to the equation and that multiplies tenfold. Here are some tips for working from home when you do not have a dedicated office:

- Invest in filing cabinets and faithfully use them. Try to have only the project you are working on out at any one time to avoid added clutter. Certain businesses are very "paperwork" heavy—for these businesses, filing systems are an absolute necessity.

- Some people have become enamored of those "console" or hutch desks, which can be closed up and shut away like an armoire at the end of the day. If you buy one of these (which can easily start at $1,000), sit yourself right down in the furniture store and really *look* at the actual work-space you will have. Very often it's extremely narrow or limited, and though an armoire may be more attractive than a desk or open shelving, if you end up working on your kitchen table because you have no elbow room, you just shelled out $1,000 for said sparse elbow room.

- Consider space in new ways. For instance, investing in a closet de-signer to overhaul a walk-in closet may yield you storage space for pa-pers, books, and office supplies that you hadn't thought of before. Carpenters can design built-in shelves or place shelving up near the ceiling. Express your needs to any professional designer or carpenter you bring into your home. They tend to "see" spatially in ways we ordi-nary mortals do not.

- When mixing home and office in small space, take special care that your kids can't get at important papers (not to mention permanent markers and your IRS returns). Consider plastic containers with labels that can be put away (up high, on shelves, in a closet) at the end of the day.

- Don't neglect ergonomics. Your spine will thank you. Often, when start-ing out and working from a space not truly "office" space, such as a kitchen table, you may be surprised to find that the heights of tables and chairs used for dining purposes are not at all well-suited to working pur-poses. When people leave a large company, for instance, they may take for granted the desk chair they had or the desk height, but office design-ers may have had a hand in selecting these items to ensure comfort. If you find yourself uncomfortable, you won't put in your most productive day. Erica's first desk space was so poorly planned in her first home that she ended up sitting on the *floor* and working on her coffee table. Her chiropractor was not amused. See the ergonomics section of this chapter for specific tips.

A Room with a Door

If you are fortunate enough to have a *real* dedicated office with a door, you can begin creating a space that reflects the office you've always wanted. We've all heard horror stories of companies where personal items are not allowed to be displayed, places with tiny cubicles, lack of storage space, and file cabinets from the 1940s. Maybe you've even worked at a place like that (we have). A dedicated office allows you to take stock of the kind of "space" you want to create. For some, this will mean being creative and colorful; for others it will mean meticulous filing systems. Either way, you're in charge.

People all over the world consider Feng Shui when designing their office spaces. Others consider natural light, whether they want a "homey" feel, or whether they wish to indulge a taste for ultramodern. For many of us, it is simply a relief to get away from the drab gray and fluorescent lights of an on-site office.

While it may seem insignificant, planning your very own office environment can actually bring great pleasure—both at the time you do it and in the long run. It's a terrific energy booster to really feel excited to get to your desk every morning. Often, new telecommuters and new entrepreneurs at home revel in the first weeks of a 60-second commute. However, you can further enhance this feeling by indulging your personality when shaping this space. Don't many people leave corporate America because they feel like a drone? A number? Well, if you want yellow walls and scented candles, posters of Jimi Hendrix on the wall, and Led Zeppelin playing in the background—it's your office! One of our favorite mottos is: *Get used to thinking like a CEO.* Design your office space for you. Be decisive and let your personality shine through.

Color: All in the Mind?

"Color psychology" is a relatively new niche within the realm of studying the mind and the mind-body connection. Interior designers and psychologists alike are studying the role of color on our moods. Certainly, when painting workspace at home, it might be helpful to consider the principles of cool versus warm and the relationship colors and hue have with our energy level. Looking at the color wheel (remember that from grade school?), you can see the relationships colors have with each other. Warm colors are thought to increase energy (oranges, reds, etc.), whereas some studies have linked cool colors with a drop in blood pressure and even with soothing behaviorally disordered children. One theory of how color reacts with the mind is that neurotransmitters in the eye transmit information about light to the brain and that this information releases a hormone that affects our mood, mental clarity, and energy level. Think of how you work best in your chosen profession. Some writers and graphic artists might prefer to be calm and serene as they create. Those in high-pressure sales positions might like feeling revved up. While the jury is out decisively on the role of color and the mind, we are all, usually, in touch with the type of color we prefer on the walls.

The Kid Zone

If you work from home with children around for part or all of the time and you have a dedicated office, you can start teaching your children that when the door is shut, they must respect that serious work is going on and that you must only be disturbed for crises. "Crises," however, has different definitions for adults and children. You might feel that a crisis means the toilet is over-flowing and flooding the bathroom. Or that two siblings are fighting a "Wrestling Deathmatch" that looks like it might lead to actual bloodshed. "Crisis," to a child, may mean the peanut butter can't be found or your child has just finished the last—the very last!—chocolate chip cookie in the Keebler bag. So good communication, just as it is in an outside office, is key. Define what crisis means and never, ever assume.

If you are fortunate enough to have an office with a door, this can help you get into the "office mindset." This can also create a mental line of demarcation between being "in the office" and being "at home." A door creates an illusion or atmosphere of professionalism and helps cut down on distractions.

On the other side of the shut-door policy can be that when the door is open, the kids are free to bother you within reason. Many parents who make the choice to work from home do so with the idea that they will be available "just for a cuddle," and that's precisely why they decided to work from home in the first place. Cuddle breaks are not part of corporate culture, but they can, wonderfully, be part of home office culture.

The other nice thing about a door is something you may not have thought of when setting up a home office: *It allows you to shut your work in.* In other words, one of the pitfalls of working from home is never leaving the office behind. Every time you walk past that desk, it's a reminder of what you've left undone. (Conversely, many home office workers have told us they feel guilty walking past piles of laundry or undone dishes. It's a double-edged sword.)

Workaholic tendencies can be very much magnified if you start your own business or work from home. Shutting the door after you physically leave the office can be a way of separating all that work from your personal life. If you are without a door, consider putting files away and not leaving them on your desk, or doing some sort of ritual that signals to your mind that the day is, indeed, over.

Now what if you do not have a door on your office and you've got those gremlins in your house? Erica doesn't have an office with a door. Her home office is set up in what used to be the dining room. Chosen for its natural light and picture windows, it is in the traffic route of the house. From there, she can keep an eye on three kids, the dogs, parakeets, rabbit, and general mayhem. A desk and fantastic shelving provide the space to work. Because she does not have a door, she instead has a sort of "code word." When she is on the telephone and cannot be interrupted, she says, "This is *business*," while giving her kids the evil eye. It doesn't work all the time, but interrupting a *busi-*

ness call to report that the rabbit is loose in the kitchen is a more serious of-fense than, say, interrupting a call to Grandma. Setting up a code word, and, for that matter, sitting down with your kids periodically and explaining what you do and why it must be quiet sometimes, is part of running a successful home office. Just as you would communicate with your peers in an office en-vironment, remember that your family, if you have one around you at home, is now part of your Board of Directors.

Honey, Stop Talking to Me

Don't have children? Spouses and significant others can be just as guilty of impinging on your time. If your spouse has the day off (or, in this day and age, if you BOTH work from home), he or she may love to wander into your work area to chat—about your mother-in-law, about the new restaurant opening up down the street, or about the fact that the refrigerator is woefully empty. One work-at-home husband put it this way, "I love that my wife and I both work at home. But there are times when our different work styles drive me crazy. When I worked outside the home, she never called me at the office with what I consider trivial problems, like what we should have for dinner, or if there was a mechanical problem with one of our appliances, or whatever. But when we're both at home, even if she's in the spare bedroom on her lap-top, she gets up frequently to just make conversation with me." Having dif-ferent work styles is again about communication and coming to some sort of middle ground. How did this couple solve their problem? They designated a "lunch hour" to take together and get all their talking out then.

Work and Play

The next decision is one specifically for those home office types with kids. You need to weigh whether your office is going to have a play area or not. For some work-at-home Moms and Dads, the office is most decidedly an of-fice. Children are free to come in and out and to draw pictures with office supplies; however, when they're in the office, in some ways it is a treat. They are in the domain of a big person, in much the same way that children who get to spend the day with Mom or Dad at an off-site office consider that spe-cial, such as "Take Your Child to Work Day."

On the other hand, some parents load a corner of the office with toys and crayons and coloring books, designating a spot for a child or children to play quietly in full view of Mom or Dad.

So which philosophy on work/play space is better?

Much like our last chapter where we discussed personality type as a factor in the home office equation, the answer to this question also takes personality into account. Ask yourself the following questions:

- Can you work with low-level but constant child noise in the background?
- Can you tolerate clutter, as in toys scattered about?
- What about your children's personalities? Will they want to be with you all the time anyway, making keeping toys handy a smart idea?
- Does your work require using expensive equipment, such as a laptop, and are your children at the "need to touch everything" stage?
- Are your children at ages when they can be quiet, if need be, for more than five minutes?

Factor in the answers to these questions as you decide whether you want your home office environment to be a sacred place for you alone, or a shared commodity.

Equipment Concerns

Technology at home is covered in the next chapter, but when it comes to equipment and gadgets, remember that you are mingling home and office. This means your equipment is exposed to certain hazards that regular on-site equipment is not. Fido or Kitty Cat jumping up and taking a nap on your keyboard. Sticky little fingers. Even your own tendency, in the home office, to relax a bit more, perhaps eat at your desk with your feet up. Also, if equipment breaks down, you now have to pay for it (or at least spend a couple of hours on the phone to technical support). There's no calling the management information systems (MIS) department and complaining that you need a replacement. Durability is important, as are good warranties. And don't forget to make sure your home or apartment insurance policy would cover the loss of equipment in the event of a robbery or flood damage . . . or cookies "fed" into the diskette drive (yes, this happened to Erica).

Storage of expensive or essential equipment is also all-important with children (and pets) around. You may think that you have hammered home to your kids *not* to touch your laptop or your diskettes. Murphy's Law applies at the home office tenfold. Locks are not a bad idea. Better to be cautious than to lose precious work to a child who means well but doesn't understand that initialing a contract in purple crayon is not what you had in mind.

Ergonomics: Keeping Comfortable in Your Home Office

Big companies spend big bucks studying ergonomics and how to avoid repetitive-motion injuries. Ergonomics is a subfield of biotechnology—those studies relating biological and engineering data to the relationship between people and machines.

What are repetitive-motion injuries? Carpal tunnel syndrome, relatively unknown until a few years ago, has not only burst into the news and lawsuits, but has spawned new equipment to help ease this injury or avoid it in the first place. If you are fortunate enough to not have this injury, you may not know that it can literally incapacitate your arm and hand in the affected side—or both right and left, though that is less common—by irritating the carpal tunnel nerve. This is most often caused by keyboarding eight hours a day or any other type of job in which someone repeats a motion all day long, or much of the day, and the nerve gets inflamed. This is just one of many repetitive motion injuries possible, depending on your job (though it is one of the most common and gets a great deal of media attention).

Are split keyboards, gel pads, and wrist braces—equipment available to try to ease strain—worth it to fend off carpal tunnel? It depends on whether you've been struck with an aching case of tendonitis or not. However, one thing no home office should be without is an ergonomic chair if you plan on spending eight hours a day or more sitting in it. Even the simplest of products can be a disaster to use if poorly designed—and nowhere is this more apparent than in chairs.

"Oh my aching back!" If this is your complaint, join the club. Estimates run as high as 80 percent of all Americans seek help for back-related injuries and aches and pains at some time or another. Persistent sitting—and in an uncomfortable chair no less—can be to blame.

Ergonomic chairs often offer lumbar support and height controls so your feet rest comfortably on the ground—or on a small stool. In the long run, if you spend a lot of time at your desk, don't neglect your back.

As for carpal tunnel and other injuries often related to word processing, such as eye strain, remember that being at home does afford you the luxury of taking a walk outside, taking an exercise break in the middle of the day, doing some yoga poses, or otherwise pampering what ails you. Remember, if you're in the middle of "Downward Facing Dog" (a yoga pose), no boss is going to wander in and wonder if you've lost your mind. Your spouse and kids may wonder, but they probably do already.

So when designing your home office, don't forget the most important worker—you. Try to design with your comfort in mind. Here are some quick tips about ergonomics:

- Buy chairs with armrests.
- Change positions frequently. Try to get up and walk around every half hour or hour.
- Frequently rotate your neck. If you keyboard for a large portion of the day, do the same with your wrists. Ask your physician for exercises that focus on "range of motion" so you can do stretching and other exercises specifically for those joints that take a repetitive beating day after day.
- Don't forget your eyes! Though you may not think of your eyes and ergonomics, remember to look out the window or at another view from time to time rather than at a screen for eight hours straight to reduce eye strain. Also, keep your screen no farther than 30 inches away from you. Don't have your screen configured in any way that requires you to look UP at it. And finally, cut glare with smart light choices as well as shades or blinds that let you block sun rays.

The 60-Second Office: Your Style

Finally, remember that your home office doesn't have to look like the CEO's of IBM. It's nice if you can have the space and equipment to feel like a "player," but you are combining the words "home" and "office." Don't feel that rattles, Barbie dolls, and Matchbox cars; your dog's rubber bones; and your golf clubs can't mingle with your papers, laptop, and diskettes. This book is designed to make you feel comfortable with the choice you personally make for you and the people in your life. We hope that reading about how someone else handles this amazing juggling act will provide some inspiration or ideas for your own circus act. If this book has inspired you to take an entrepreneurial step and set up a business from home, or to finally get up the nerve to ask your boss if you can telecommute, terrific. If you have to start from your kitchen table, you won't be the first. Remember, though, even on your worst day in the home office—you only had to commute 60 seconds!

CHAPTER **3**

TECHNOLOGY: 60-SECOND COMMUTE ESSENTIALS

Welcome to the age of technology. There has never been a better time to work from home. Even the catchword "telecommuting" was born of technology.

All home office professionals need equipment. Depending on what it is you do, technology needs can range from fax machines to copiers, computers to data storage. When trying to combine a family into the home office equation, choices in equipment become more urgent. You need equipment that will stand up to sticky little fingers or peanut butter smears. Erica has one darling who fed Cheerios into the disk drive of her computer.

If you're a telecommuter, your company may provide you with some or all of the equipment you need to "hook up" to the on-site office (though this varies from company to company). But if you're starting a home-based business, you may be worried about keeping costs low as you invest in equipment to get your company up and running.

And what about all the bells and whistles? Technology can easily become its own monster with so many gadgets and electronics you almost don't know where to turn first. Admittedly, too, some of us are "gadget geeks" who just can't live without all the latest electronic marvels. We see it in the computer store or eye our friend using it and just have to have it. But is having every gadget necessary, and is the cost and time taken to learn all the equipment's capabilities really worth it?

This chapter will then cover some of the basics of home office equipment. For starters, Cheerios in a disk drive *will* render said disk drive unusable.

Equipment and Gadgets

When it comes to equipment and gadgets, remember that you are mingling home and office. This means your equipment is exposed to certain hazards that regular on-site equipment is not. Durability is important. Don't forget to make sure your home or apartment insurance policy would cover the loss of equipment in the event of a robbery or flood damage (for more information, see our insurance chapter).

Remember the MIS department? In most companies they are a godsend—and a bane. Maybe you remember complaining that they weren't "getting around" to fixing the gremlin in your office computer fast enough. Well, guess what? Unless you're a telecommuter, if equipment breaks down, you now have to pay for it (or at least spend a couple of hours on the phone to an 800-number). There's no calling the MIS department and complaining that you need a replacement. The first time you have a computer-related fiasco on your hands, you're going to miss those MIS people! Ensure you don't have a double disaster on your hands by investing in good warranties. These can cover anything from repairs to replacement, and they are essential for home office technology. A glass of chocolate milk poured over your laptop by your two-year-old darling? One, that's what they make spill-proof sippy cups for. Two, thank goodness you have that covers-everything-under-the-sun warranty.

As we pointed out in the last chapter, another wise home office investment is storage such as filing cabinets, an armoire, or locking trunk—anything where you can tuck away your work at the end of the day. This, again, helps with that "line of demarcation." Your personal life and work life may blur a bit more in the home office, so shutting down and literally putting things away at the end of the day can help you "leave" the office, even if that office is a few steps away.

Storage is also all-important with children (and pets) around. One safety warning: Filing cabinets are notoriously unstable. If two drawers are pulled out and you have a child who decides to go "climbing," this is a hospital emergency visit waiting to happen. Keep file drawers closed.

A Word About Cellphones

We know that cellphones are all the rage. Pretty soon, some say, we won't use land-lines, just our cellphones. But please use cellphones with caution. By that we mean please don't drive and talk on your cellphone at the same time. We realize the temptation to do so is strong; "everyone" does it. But car accidents happen with more frequency when drivers are distracted by their phone calls. We suggest that you view your cellphone as a fabulous "waiting room tool." By this we mean that when you are safely out of your car, but find yourself waiting in a dentist's office, at your child's soccer practice, or in the drive-thru line at the bank, that you can use your cellphone then to return quick phone calls. This is a good time to call people you know are not available but for whom you wish to leave messages or voicemails, to make appointments, or to check on the status of something—any quick call that you can strike off your To-Do list using time that is typically wasted waiting around. Many counties in the United States now forbid them when driving anyway (Kathy's hometown does). At the *very least*, get a hands-free attachment.

Here are a few ideas and suggestions regarding home office equipment and gadgets:

- You cannot skimp on your answering machine/voice mail. If you are trying to present a professional image, whether running a carpet-cleaning franchise or a small accounting office, there is nothing worse than someone calling and hearing a semi-warped taped message that sounds like static. It makes people feel uneasy, as if they're leaving a message for someone who may—or may not—return their call.

- Do not skimp on warranties, surge protection, virus scans, and disk backup space (such as Zip drives and CD-ROMs) if you use a computer. Remember, when you worked in a corporate environment, very often an MIS department backed up the whole "system" at night when you went home. You need to foresee computer disasters and be prepared for them (that also means backing up your work frequently and defragging your computer on a routine basis).

- Do skimp on bells and whistles. While a personal digital assistant like a Palm Pilot® may be really cool and may in fact be extremely useful, if you are concerned about start-up costs, it is something a desk planner system under $100 can do if used faithfully. The same goes for other bells and whistles items like a built-in DVD player on a laptop. Nice . . . but do you *have* to have it?

- Speaking of bells and whistles . . . if you *do* purchase a personal digital assistant or software to input your clients' information and so on, you may find that you end up spending an exorbitant amount of your precious time learning how to use it and use it effectively. And for all that effort, many people also come to discover they only use about 1/100th of the digital equipments' capabilities. For instance, we have a friend who works from home and has a Palm Pilot. Recently, this friend confessed she only used the digital assistant as a glorified electronic address book. Before you purchase a personal digital assistant (PDA) or other "gadget"-oriented item, gauge your own personality, such as aptitude for electronics. Many people swear by their PDA, but purchase one only if you know that, deep down, you're really going to use it successfully.

25

- Envision success, and buy for it ahead of time if you can afford it. For example, you may not think, initially, that you need software to electronically keep track of all your clients' addresses, phone numbers, likes and preferences, and orders. You may think to yourself, *I only have 10 clients . . . I can remember most of that in my head. I don't need the software.* Fast forward six months when you are busy beyond belief and that client list has grown to 100. Now you may find yourself facing a truly aggravating and business-halting period of time making the changeover to the very software you could have used right from the start.

- While it may not technically fall under the heading of gadgets, don't forget all the little supplies. We take for granted, in the corporate office environment, that we will have just the right-sized rubber band, paper clip, or file folder. We assume we have an unlimited supply of Wite-Out®, pens, paper, and laser cartridges. Take it from us, when you are trying to print out a 100-page document at the zero hour, FedEx® is on its way, you're barely going to make the five o'clock deadline, and you run out of ink in your printer AND you don't have a spare cartridge, you—and your client—are not going to be happy.

- Don't skimp on organizational materials that work for *you*. Most home office professionals wear many hats, including accountant, marketing wiz, secretary, and even cleaning crew. The only way we have found to make this manageable is by being organized. If organization isn't your strong suit, pay close attention to the organization chapter. We can help you. Trust us.

- Look into products that do more than one function. Some laser printers function as copiers and fax machines. Some scanners function as copiers. Some computer systems allow you to send faxes via e-mail. In other words, with limited space and budget in the home office, products that also multitask (just like you!) are a good choice.

- Do your research on multitasking products. We have heard, in our research, stories of people who were displeased with the fax capabilities of a printer, or the copying capabilities of a scanner, for example. When purchasing equipment, it's wise to consider those that are going to get the most use. For instance, Erica never thought she needed a dedicated fax because of extensive e-mail use in the publishing industry. However, over time, it has become one of the more-used pieces of equipment. Now she regrets not investing in a better fax, one that doesn't jam each time she tries to fax more than 10 pages at a time.

- When making big-budget technology decisions, ask friends and colleagues for personal recommendations. Find out what they like—and don't like—about their printer, PDA, or laptop. If you can't get reliable recommendations, purchase magazines tailored to the PC or computer industry, or home office industry, and read up on the latest and greatest to find out if products live up to their price tag.

- Don't forget software. The latest version of Windows XP® has security features that detect if you bootleg a copy. While many people rely on bootleg copies of software from the Internet or burned CDs from friends and family, you may, depending on your company, have to invest in software to run it. You may also have to invest in software you've never used before. For instance, suppose you're a PR executive and you use Microsoft Word for Windows to write your PR pieces. You've planned for that. However, you may have to invest in accounting software to run an actual company from home.

- When considering whether to have a separate phone line for your business, take into account the cost versus the inconvenience of fighting for the existing home line with other members of your household.

- If you DO share a phone line with the household, voice mail built-in to your phone system (i.e., available through your phone carrier) is an ideal solution. You can have a message that says "Push 1 for Tom, 2 for Dick, and 3 for Harry." The advantage is not having to rely on family members to take messages. Have the household learn to let the machine pick up during business hours if you are not available, and have the capability to have the message play if you are on the other line.

- If you're a telecommuter, you will need to coordinate with the on-site office on issues of technological compatibility.

Communication Lines: The 'Net and Phones

Talking on the Go

Not everyone starting a business from home has the resources to immediately buy such higher-end business equipment as computers, faxes, copying machines, and so forth. However, we will let you in on a secret: The most valuable single piece of office equipment you can buy—especially if you're a parent with kids underfoot—is a portable phone or a headset.

That's right. For under $100 you can buy a portable phone that will enable you to roam through your home. This, we assure you, is the only way work and kids can be under the same roof. It allows you to duck your head into the family room to make sure your children aren't hanging from the rafters while you've been quietly working on a grant proposal on PowerPoint®, which you are now discussing with your client.

A portable phone also allows you to find a quiet nook if need be. If you are not fortunate enough to be able to have a dedicated office, and you need to talk to a client or customer and want to sound totally professional without background chatter, the bathroom or even a closet can become your own personal corporate kingdom. We both have made many a phone call from the privacy and quiet (and locked door!) of the bathroom, walk-in closet, or whatever hideout was available.

No kids at home? A portable phone still lets you roam the house. Maybe for you, one of the reasons working from home is so attractive is you gain the ability to do a few household chores during the day and cut down on all the stuff you have to do at night. A portable phone, and most especially a hands-free headset, is a treasure—and one most home office workers can't live without.

E-mail

Most businesses today cannot survive without e-mail. When you work in an on-site office, e-mail is taken for granted. You log in, plug in your password, and there are your messages. When setting up a business at home, the e-mail question becomes more involved. You need to decide how you're going to access the Internet and what provider you are going to use.

For telecommuters, some of these questions regarding the Internet may be predefined by the company for which you work. If not, you still need to answer the same questions of reliability, speed, and access.

When most people started logging onto the Internet in the 1990s (although the Internet has been around much longer, most people didn't begin using it as a primary form of communication until much more recently), the choice of what method to get your connection was pretty much through the telephone line. Though some people who worked for the

The origins of the Internet were a joint venture by the Department of Defense and research universities to share scientific and technological information.

government may have had access to DSL lines or more sophisticated technology, most of us "regular folk" logged on with painfully slow modems connected through our phone line.

The technological landscape has changed, and now you can log onto the Internet in a variety of ways. When logging on from home, you need to pick the one that best suits your needs.

Cable Modem: This modem allows you to access the Internet through your cable line. It also requires an alteration in your computer that your cable company will install (usually called a "surfboard"). Like DSL, it is very fast. It is, in practice, fairly reliable, but when cable is "out" and looking like snow on your TV screen, your Internet connection may be out, too. The great thing about a cable modem is that it doesn't tie up a phone line. A minus? It is more expensive per month than a dial-up server through your phone line. The cable company will also, if you "network" more than one computer in your house to the cable hook-up, want to charge you *per* computer. It can get pricey.

DSL: Digital subscriber lines (DSL) transmit over copper lines and require that you be a certain distance from a DSLAM (a type of master equipment). What this translates to is about a third of all people cannot get DSL service (Navas, TechTV.com., 2/6/01). What DSL does offer is lightning-fast connections and better reliability. As far as start-up costs, like a cable modem, your computer will need a type of "card" to connect to DSL and this requires an initial outlay of a couple hundred dollars, but for many, fast reliable service is more than worth it.

Phone Lines: Phone lines remain the most common way to get Internet access. If you only have a single line for your business, you have to think about how much of your business day you're on-line. If you spend more than a set amount of time on-line (say, a half hour), what happens to callers of your business? Will they get a busy signal? This, then, ties into your answering machine. If you have one through your phone company that will go on when the line is busy, this concern isn't so worrisome, and you can retrieve your voicemail when you log off-line. The plus side to a phone-line dial-up server is that it is inexpensive. A minus, besides blocking your phone line use if you have only one line, is that during peak "traffic" hours, you may find you reach a "busy" signal when you try to log on, or, alternatively, you may literally be knocked off-line by the heavy traffic.

ISDN: Integrated Services Digital Network (ISDN) is a service provided by local telephone companies. By modifying regular telephone lines, ISDN allows you to transmit data significantly faster than even the fastest regular or analog modems. If you regularly handle large files, ISDN or other broadband-type services like it become something most of us impatient people can't live without. For techno-junkies, ISDN lets you transmit data, voice, and video simultaneously on one line. All this sounds fast and technologically advanced. Those are the pluses. The minuses include it not being available everywhere and high start-up costs because you need your telephone company or other provider to make the adjustments to your phone line to allow it. Some truly technically proficient gurus can handle some of that themselves and reduce some of those costs. But if you're like Erica or Kathy . . . you need someone to do it for you.

Wireless: Are we reaching the wireless age? Someday, as we said in our discussion of cell phones, we may abandon "land lines" entirely. We'll all be wireless and utilizing satellites to transmit our information, talk on the phone, and download data from anywhere in the world. We'll be truly portable in our technology, able to take our technology with us as we travel, and will not worry about "connections." Wireless technology for Internet hook-up is still a smaller segment of the business pie right now. It is more expensive—a minus. However, you can be connected almost anywhere (great for travelers) and it is fast—the pluses.

Internet Provider: Who shall you choose as your Internet provider? All of the aforementioned methods will provide access to the Internet, but then you still need to pay for a provider who, in a sense, "organizes" that access and allows you to "surf the 'Net." Some people, particularly the technically proficient, will access free providers. Some services will let you get e-mail for free . . . but again, how will you surf the 'Net? America Online (AOL) remains the most popular provider. However, some people have access problems with a busy signal preventing them from logging on at peak times. A plus is that AOL really does have graphics and services aligned in such a way that you could be virtually computer illiterate and still understand what to do to get your mail, surf the 'Net, add a "bookmark" (noting where some of your favorite sites are) and so on. We could fill a book with all the alternatives to AOL. Erica uses Netscape, for instance, and a cable modem hookup. The main questions are ease of access, how technically proficient (or not) you are, and finally, what sort of files and data you deal with. Some providers do not allow file transfers beyond a certain size. So, consider what you use your access for. E-mail only? Data transfer? Internet research and search engines? Answer these questions and you will be able to narrow your choice of provider.

How Many Lines?: How many lines do you need? It depends on who's vying for the phone line, how much time you spend on-line, whether you're going to have a dedicated fax line, and whether or not callers will get a busy signal if they call your house and someone (you or a family member) is already using the line.

Confused about what configuration to choose?: Don't be. While it can be a pain to switch, there's always the option of starting out with something you feel comfortable with, and then switching to more high-tech methods as you become more computer-literate and savvy as a home-based office worker. On the flip side, if you can envision the needs of your business and buy ahead for different eventualities, save yourself the headaches and do so.

Instant Messaging

Instant messaging (IM) software allows workers (and friends) to communicate in real time. For teams of telecommuters or combined teams of on-site and off-site workers, they can communicate with the convenience of e-mail, in real time, but with less hassle than playing phone tag.

One of the negatives of the IM world, however, is its abuse. You know . . . the person who uses IM as a personal "chatroom" and can't seem to get off of it and get to work. Just as we have e-mail "rules of the road," heed these for using IM:

- IM does have an "Audit Trail" feature that will let you track conversations. However, IM should never be used for very important requests. It's too easy for the message to get ignored or lost.

- IM is best for short answers to quick queries.

- IM is not an e-mail replacement.

- Use IM icons such as "Busy" or "Do not disturb" to let other workers know whether you're available or not.

- Don't abuse IM as a personal chit-chat tool. It's too distracting for others.

If you've been used to a computer at a job and are now seeking to buy one on your own, here are some common computer terminology definitions to get you started as you comparison shop.

CPU: Stands for central processing unit. It's the "guts" of your computer.

Monitor: Aim for the biggest one you can afford, especially if you are going to spend a large portion of your day on the computer. Prices have come down considerably.

RAM: Random access memory. How much do you store on your hard drive? The more you store, and the more programs you run—particularly memory-intensive ones, for instance, like HTML or Flash (web design) programs—the more RAM memory you need.

Hard Drive Memory: Different from RAM. These are the physical hard disks that actually hold the programs and the data. You can have more than one of them, and now that the prices have trickled down, you can buy many gigabytes of hard disk memory for a fraction of what such internal storage capacity once cost.

Zip drive: A Zip can hold about 100 megabytes of information. A Zip drive is used, most often, for backing up critical files and for transferring files from one computer to another. (An alternative to the ZIP drive is a JAZZ drive, for which the disks hold almost a gigabyte of memory.)

Laptop or Desktop?

We are often asked about our computer equipment. While having both a laptop and a desktop would be ideal, not everyone has the money for both. Here are some pros and cons of laptop versus desktop as your *primary* computer:

- A laptop is portable, allowing you to experience the "great outdoors" or any external situation while still working. This may have been one of the "perks" you thought of when deciding to work at home. One client of Erica's commented that he hears birds in the background whenever they speak. Imagine the pleasure of working on your patio in spring, or in any setting you find enjoyable. Even in bed on a day you just don't feel like making the 60-second commute! You can take it on a plane, to the waiting room at a child's doctor's appointment, or virtually anywhere. (However, Erica recently read about a computer repair company that found small hermit crabs in a laptop from a beachgoing technophile. Not healthy for the laptop!)

- A laptop, given the aforementioned, is decidedly more vulnerable to being dropped, a catastrophe with water, or a coffee mug spilled on it, and so forth.

- A laptop, being less durable, always needs (trust us) an extended warranty plan covering breakage.

- If your laptop is your primary computer, keyboard size and screen size can be skimpy compared to a big 17-inch or greater monitor (though larger keys and monitors are available—sometimes making them heavier). If you primarily write or do a lot of keying, you may feel "clumsy" on the smaller-sized laptop keyboard. Erica, as primarily an author and novelist, abandoned her first laptop for precisely this reason. Laptop sizes do allow more freedom of choice now, and you can pay for a larger screen and so on. If budget is a concern though, you may not get the features you want as compared to a desktop.

  One of the best tech sites on the Internet that can answer all your questions—and usually in straightforward enough language that non-techies can understand—is www.techtv.com

- Desktops allow you to have every bell and whistle, including flat screens and very large monitors that are easy on the eye.

- Desktops can be ergonomically altered so you don't strain your wrists or eyes if you spend a lot of time on the computer.

60-Second Technology: Bumps in the Road

Technology can make some people feel very excited. You know those techno-lovers. They've got every gadget, every piece of software, and so on. For others, technology decisions can be a cringe-inducing experience. When considering technology in the home office, try to reduce it to questions about usage and then equip yourself with those answers as you begin shopping or setting up your office. For instance:

- How much will I use this piece of equipment?

- Am I comfortable downloading my own programs and software?

- Will I need a class to learn how to use this piece of technology or am I comfortable with my knowledge level?

- Will this gadget really be utilized to its fullest capabilities?

How much RAM? How much memory? When purchasing a computer, the tendency is to go for as much "power" as you possibly can. The thinking is that you don't want to "outgrow" your computer too quickly. In the fast-paced world of technology, computers get "dated" pretty quickly. One way to help you figure out the answer to these questions is to calculate how much RAM/memory your main programs take up and then go from there. But another important rule to follow when working from home is not to store everything on your hard drive. Crashes happen and you need to remember to back up and store files elsewhere. True "disaster planning," just like in a large company, entails storing your backup off-site in case of fire, flood, or catastrophe.

Gauging these answers and keeping in mind usage and your kind of business will help you from making costly mistakes. For example, Erica knows one man who has the most elaborate computer known to man. He brags about its RAM, its hard drive, and its flat screen. And what does he use it for? To play solitaire mostly. Consider your needs *before* you buy, and once you do settle on choices, try to familiarize yourself with those components you truly need to function to your fullest in the home office.

CHAPTER 4

THE 24/7 LIFESTYLE:
TIME MANAGEMENT IN THE HOME OFFICE

If you used to (or still do) work in an office five days a week, you probably worked from nine to five or some variation of that, and perhaps worked overtime as necessary or brought work home to review at night. Alas, for the American worker, we don't do siestas, and we don't stroll into the office at ten o'clock—on a good day—like some of our European counterparts. Even the term "24/7" is uniquely American. Between beepers and cell phones, lap top computers and e-mail, it seems we're often expected to work around the clock, and to be accessible at any hour, day or night.

Enter the home office. Now we have an entirely new concept of "the office." With this home office and the 24/7 nature of life, let's explore how to manage those 24 hours in a day when your desk is just a 60-second commute away.

Time . . . Where Does It Go?

Just as in the corporate office, where a busy morning will make the day fly by, the workday in a home office disappears into a vortex of time. From the moment each of the authors wakes up, to long after everyone else goes to bed, we're on the move.

Mornings, for us, are the off-to-school rush, and our days are filled with high-intensity work plus all the errands and chores of an average family. We can go from the "high" of sealing a big deal to the mind-numbing boredom of folding laundry in 60 seconds flat, because all that housework is just a step away. Because neither of us typically gets eight hours of uninterrupted work time, let alone the 10 or more hours professionals sometimes need when work piles up, we have to go back to "the office" after dinner or after

The American work week isn't really 40 hours at all. Despite computers and technology, which were supposed to help us cut down on our time in the office, the average work week creeps upward and upward. According to a study by the National Sleep Foundation, the average U.S. employee works a 46-hour work week. And a whopping 38 percent of U.S. workers clock in at more than 50 hours a week.

our kids are in bed. We have to find this extra time, and coffee has become a nocturnal mainstay.

Don't get us wrong: We appreciate that the home office allows us a unique advantage to choose hours that work for us, or to sometimes work these late hours when family demands dictate that we do. We're not alone in dividing up our time, either. In interviewing people for this book, we found many compatriots who split their days because of children and spouses, or caretaking elderly parents. We also found a majority who had to work late hours because the "home" in the home office equation pressed in on their work time and they had to make up for that. Many people discover being a home office worker can mean a heavier schedule than they imagined when they set up that office in the spare bedroom. You can guard against this with good time management skills and being organized from the very beginning.

Organized from the Start

While we cover organization skills and ideas in the next chapter, precious time can be wasted by lack of organization. One tip we want to pass on here, though, is to try to envision organization in your home office from the very start. If you already have a home office established, you may want to spend the time to implement these ideas, because in the long run, they will shave minutes and more off your workday.

- Set up a FedEx, UPS®, or overnight carrier service account if you ever use them for your business. Spend 15 minutes on the phone or on-line *once*, get your account, have them ship supplies right to your doorstep, and you won't have to waste time again. Don't ever sit "on hold" with FedEx or any of the other carriers. Once you are set up, you can do it all on-line, efficiently and quickly—that includes scheduling pickup, tracking packages, and ordering supplies.

- Have a postage scale and postage supplies on hand so you don't waste time on line at the post office. Again, go to the post office *once* and get all the supplies you need, along with rate sheets, and you won't have to waste time there again. This is especially important in the months of November and December, and around the dreaded income tax deadline date in April when lines at the post office are at their longest.

- Consider, depending on your mail volume and the nature of your business, getting a postage machine for bulk mail.

- Consider paying your bills on-line.

- Organize your filing cabinets and shelving systems from the start so information is at your fingertips.

- Whatever office supplies you use, keep them well-stocked so you don't run out at deadline time.

- If you regularly send clients flowers, establish an account at a florist you can trust and pre-select choices that you like. Or set up an account online at one of the national florist companies.

Body Clock Blues: Beating Them through Time Management

One of the best things about working from home is that you can adapt your work routine to your body clock. While we understand that telecommuters often must be at a desk during the business hours of their in-office counterparts, home office entrepreneurs gain a degree of flexibility.

Respecting your internal body clock means not taking a lunch hour at noon because the rest of the world is taking a lunch hour at noon. Some days you may be hungry for lunch at 11:00 A.M. Some days at 3:00 P.M. Body clock means freedom to powernap and freedom to take a time-out at 2:30 P.M. to greet the kids as they walk through the door after school and then not return to the home office until 7:00 P.M. It can mean the freedom to work out when the gym is less crowded, to take a break to do yoga, or hit the golf course. It can mean taking off a half-day every Monday to do volunteer work or pursue a hobby or dream, or hitting the tennis court each Wednesday with your old college roommate, and then working an hour extra each of the other weekdays.

However, many of us have been slaves to the nine-to-five world for so long that we aren't even sure what our body clock is telling us. Working from home means it's time to get in tune with yourself. Let go of the world's regimentation and figure out what your work hours are going to be so you are at your peak performance.

Most people know whether they are "early birds" or "night owls." Or do they? One way to discover your true body clock is to look at your sleeping, eating, and alertness patterns on the weekend. When do you feel at your brightest? When do you sense your energy is sagging? If weekends are equally full of kids' soccer games, errands, and early-rising, but you wonder if perhaps you would do better by rising *very* early and napping later in the day, you can experiment. Or, watch your body clock on vacation. Though vacation often brings with it excess, often people (especially parents) are surprised to find that even when they *can* sleep in, their eyes open by 7:00 A.M. anyway.

Another method to determine your true body clock is to closely examine your energy levels during a typical workday. When you find yourself combating fatigue at the same time each day, when you work from home you can schedule yourself a coffee break, a short snooze, or 20 minutes of yoga or walking. Take advantage of you being the boss—anything is possible.

Java Jolts

Whether you've decided to do a home office fulltime, halftime or sometime, another question you need to ask yourself is what working from home means to you? What kinds of time sacrifices are you willing to make? Does being home with your children mean you are willing to work at night? What does working from home do to your social schedule, entertaining, or what you call "your time"? If you're not a night owl by nature, can coffee or exercise help you adjust your body clock? Are you willing to work at night?

Just as in a corporate office, time management might mean having to attend a meeting instead of getting in a few hours on a pressing project, working from home necessitates flexibility. It helps you feel less frustrated by these kinds of sacrifices if you can remember times when a long-winded supervisor kept everyone in a meeting or the office gossip trapped you in the hallway to discuss the latest scuttlebutt. Time is managed—and wasted—in both corporate and home offices. Personally, we'd rather "waste" time having a chocolate chip cookie and story time break than another meeting with 10 colleagues talking and no one truly listening . . . and nothing productive really getting done besides griping.

Perhaps the home office is a way for you to exercise at a certain time each day, or to schedule a tee-time at the golf course. Maybe it lets you pursue an avocation. If so, see how time sacrifices here and there can help you achieve those goals. Remember to think outside the box as far as time goes. You may be surprised that many little chunks of time can actually add up to a true 40-hour workweek. Jessica Stasinos, an indexer and publishing professional, works during her son's nap time and late at night. It adds up to over a 30-hour week but is broken up entirely and never in one fell swoop. "I made this decision," she says, "and I budget my time accordingly."

Telecommuters vocally reminded us during the writing of the book that sometimes they don't have such choices. They may need to be in a home office for very specific hours corresponding to those employees in the office. However, even in cases where hours must conform to an office, having access to your files, computer, and so forth at night and in the early morning may allow windows of more *relaxed* time during the day. In any case, examine your motives for working from home and know that sometimes the best-laid plans go awry. When that happens, there's always caffeine and working 'til midnight. As one telecommuter recently told us, "I had planned to work this evening, but my husband had to stay late at the law office, leaving me to do bedtimes and bath. I'll be working late. Bring on the coffee."

Quiet Time

When you work in an office outside the home, you rarely have to factor in noise-level considerations in the course of the day. When you work from home, you're part of the home office family. You are part of a living organism, in a way. Every household has a rhythm, has times when the house is quiet, and times when it is bursting at the seams. You need to learn those rhythms and think about them as you make decisions about scheduling your day.

Typically, children are quiet in the morning. In the afternoons, everyone has cabin fever, or the kids are coming home from school and need to let loose with their energy for a little while. Therefore, phone calls become more thought-out. If you worked in a corporate environment, you probably never gave a thought to picking up the phone when it rang or returning calls at any particular time of the day. In a home office, phone calls may need to be returned in the family's downtime.

Even those without kids may find their dogs bark incessantly at the mail carrier at noon each day. (Erica's dog has an intense hatred, bordering on psychopathy, of the man in the brown UPS truck!) If you live in the city, in an apartment building, you may discover the garbage trucks roll at an inconvenient time or your neighbor upstairs practices his off-key clarinet at 11:00 each morning.

We found some 60-second commuters have the opposite problem—it's *too* quiet. When making the transition from an office to home, the silence may actually take some getting used to. For instance, if you are used to chatter, phones ringing, faxes rolling, printers spouting out pages, and so on in a corporate environment, the sudden silence of being home alone, especially if you are home alone all the time, may make it hard to concentrate.

In *Creating Emotionally Safe Schools* (HCI, Inc.), Jane Bluestein, an educational specialist and author, discusses how as children we learn in different fashions: Some learn by having background music, some by lying on the floor, others by having complete silence. As adults, we're probably still "hard-wired" in much the same way. We're sure you know people who work best with music playing and others who shut their office doors and demand silence. One of our clients has CNN running at a fairly high audible volume in his office at all times. Another client wears headphones with relaxing classical music. Regardless of your style, getting used to the quiet—or planning for it if you have kids or other noise—may be a factor you need to consider in your time management at home.

Voice Mail

While voice mail systems are covered in our technology chapter, it pays to remember that investing in a professional voice mail system or answering machine is a wise expenditure for the home office. If the household is noisy, don't try to carry on a conversation. Return the call when things settle down. You may play phone tag, but it's better than shouting over the noise. Today, with voice mail available through the phone company, or good machines offering quality sound, you can come across as very much the professional from the confines of your home. There is even a new service that makes it sound as if you have a virtual "receptionist." Don't feel compelled to pick up the telephone if a baby is crying or a dog is barking in the background for instance. Use voice mail and call when the atmosphere at home is more conducive to conducting business.

Shutting the Door, Even if You Don't Have One

Even if your home office doesn't have a door, time management has to include shutting the proverbial door. By this we mean that the temptation to lose a sense of boundaries in a home office is very real. This is two-fold.

In family situations, on the one hand, having access to you at all hours can mean your family intrudes on you so much that you find yourself stretched to your limit. On the other hand, with an office *always* there, especially if the business is your own and you feel the pressure of financially needing to make a success of your home-based venture, the temptation can be to work 24/7. Time management means, impossible as it may sometimes seem, finding time for yourself and remembering that shutting the door, or shutting your eyes and ignoring the pile of work on your desk, is both healthy and necessary.

You need to remind yourself that you are one person. You need to have a life. You deserve one. Shut the door. Turn off the computer. Go for a walk in the fresh air. *Tell your clients your office hours and stick to them.*

Time Management in Your Personal Life

We have an entire chapter on organizing your life, from paperclips to your taxes. However, in time management, we need to give a nod to managing time between your work and personal life.

First, we are both big believers (bordering on evangelical fervor!) in day planner systems. There are many name brands out there, and they all offer add-ons and calendars that help particular businesses from telecommuters to salespersons who get car mileage allowances to those who travel and must prepare expense accounts. The organization chapter covers how to use these scheduling systems to your best advantage. Other workers favor "To-Do" lists. Still others advocate electronic and computerized scheduling systems. In terms of time management, your best defense against a day spent under the gun is careful planning—the night before. Getting your new day off on the right foot means looking at your obligations the evening before and having a game plan. Even 15 minutes the night before can save you precious time the next day.

In addition, if you're trying to juggle telecommuting or a home-based business with a full family life, it pays to think how you can get ahead of that game and save yourself time in the long run. Whether it's stocking up on greeting cards and wrapping paper, planning meals in advance instead of five minutes before everyone starts complaining they're hungry, or configuring the laundry area for optimal efficiency, running your household smoothly will only help you run your business more smoothly.

Even those without children or family living at home fall prey to the errand demon. Errands are consistently named the worst "time waster," so planning routes, paying on-line and having on-line banking, and other ideas to cut back on errands will pay off with more precious minutes in your workweek.

> Save yourself time and energy by purchasing several birthday presents at the same time. If you think something is a great buy, then get three or four of them. That way you always have extra presents on hand if you're in a crunch. Top this off with a variety of gift paper and all-occasion cards. We advocate doing things once and stocking up or planning ahead.

"Plan B": When a Good Day Goes Bad— Very Bad

When you work from home, you need to be prepared for the unexpected. For example, you plan out a quiet workday because the kids are in school until three o'clock. An hour later, the school nurse is calling because one of your children is throwing up. Next thing you know, your perfect day is over and you are in the car driving to your child's school.

Successfully working from a home office depends on you being able to roll with the unforeseen surprises that will occur. If you are the rigid type or have a tendency to come undone when things don't go your way, you will be very cranky at worst—and most certainly not your most productive at best.

Try to have a "Plan B" for various home office disasters. Even for telecommuters, and those without kids, disaster on the home front can mean a lost workday. For instance, you may not have children, but that doesn't mean you won't find yourself spending half a day waiting for a car to be repaired when you were told it would only take an hour. Or that you won't suddenly have a personal emergency, trip to the dentist that turns into a root canal, and so forth. A "Plan B" enables you to salvage part of your day. For instance, we have a client who is never without her day planner. If she has to get her car repaired or go to the doctor's office, she brings it along and uses waiting room time and excessive delays to organize even *months* in advance. John Diaz, a salesman, is a firm believer in sending personal note cards to clients for holidays and thank yous. He keeps a supply of them in his glove compartment and uses stalled traffic, waiting for the oil to be changed in his mechanic's waiting area, and other typical "time wasters" as a way to maximize his day.

For those with children, sickness tends to be the ultimate "Plan B" crisis. Keep the items on the list below on hand for days when you're child is home from school. It's also good idea to have the necessary medications available (i.e., Tylenol, cough medicines, etc.) so that you don't have to go running out to the drugstore with a sick child in tow. Remember, again, if you buy two or three of a common item (such as Tylenol or cough syrup) *once*, you will be saved a trip somewhere down the road that will, because of Murphy's Law, come at the most inconvenient time possible. The items on this list below can amuse a sick child so he or she doesn't demand all of your attention:

Movies
Puzzles
Coloring books
CD games

It pays to have some of these be NEW items. Why? Who doesn't like something new? A new CD-ROM game is going to amuse your child a whole lot more than one that's been played a thousand times before.

Next, figure out what you can do in the moments your child is feeling needy or wants you close at hand. You can straighten up, sort the mail, and so forth—versus what you can do later on when your child is sleeping.

Plan B is like any office emergency system—the more prepared you are for any eventuality, the more likely it is you will not lose an entire day of work.

Top Five Time Wasters

- Telephone calls (that's what Caller ID is for!)
- E-mails (get off everyone's joke lists)
- Interruptions
- Messy work area
- Lack of a schedule

Top Ten T-i-m-e S-t-r-e-t-c-h-e-r-s

- Keep an organized work area so you don't waste time hunting for things.
- Plan your day ahead of time, and set yourself up the night before.
- Keep your To-Do lists short and realistic for each day (e.g., the top two or three things you must do that day).
- Before you take on something new, like a new commitment or exercise class, eliminate something old or that you don't need/want anymore.
- Group tasks together (e.g., all errands, calls, paperwork, reading, filing).
- Screen your phone calls with an answering machine or caller ID.
- Use a hands-free head set so that you can do two things at once.
- Use down time or "waiting room" time for planning and reorganizing, catching up on reading, and so forth.
- Write down a phone memo with date, time, and reason for calling and record it in one place.
- Do your hardest work during your peak hours.

Bargaining in the Home Office Boardroom

Here's a tip for those with kids at home. Whether you bring home a brief-case full of work you must finish up or you work from home full-time, in-evitably you feel the push and pull of demands on your time. We have found that when the children are clamoring for your attention, there really is little point in yelling at them or time-outs. Remember the days when you bargained in the boardroom? The same holds true in the home office. Sometimes, a simple egg timer can be a saving grace. Set if for 20 minutes and explain that you will read a story, relax with them, dance to their favorite CD with them—whatever they want—the 20 minutes is theirs. Your part of the bargain is you cannot answer the phone or do anything on your desk. The idea is to make the children feel as important to you as that briefcase full of work. For them, sometimes the Attention Monster is simply about knowing they are important to you—as important as your beeper, your phone, your computer, or your desk of papers.

In return, when the timer goes off, they must give you 20 minutes of total peace. Let them take the timer into another room and busy themselves until it goes off. While this may seem like a very simple solution, it really does work. In fact, it works so well, you may ask, Why didn't *I* think of it before?

Why does it work? Saying to a child, "I need to get this done . . . I need some time right now," doesn't give them anything measurable. It is vague. The timer gives them a measurable unit of time. By also playing for 20 min-utes first, you have soothed them at a time when they really felt they needed you; consequently, they feel more secure. The amazing thing about this is that often, when they go away for "your" 20 minutes, they get so caught up in something new they forget all about the time limit. *But appeasing them, bargaining in your own boardroom, is part of the give and take of time manage-ment at home.*

Time Management and Productivity

When you work in a corporate environment, you are at the mercy of every-one else's schedule. The department head calls a meeting at 11:00 A.M., which happens to be your most "up" time of day, when you like to do sales calls. But you dutifully head to the meeting because it's mandatory.

Just as we suggest looking at your body clock to take advantage of some freedom from the nine-to-five rut, we also suggest looking at your time man-agement in terms of productivity. Tedious tasks should be done when you are most tired. File when you feel you need to give your brain some downtime, not when you are at your peak. If you feel lonely and want to take time to make a phone call to a client you usually enjoy talking to, make the call when you need an energy lift. Save your peak performance times for those tasks that require your peak performance.

Only 24 Hours in a Day: Overbooking Time

There are only 24 hours in a day. We know it. You know it. So why do our day planners sometimes look as if there are 72 hours in a day? We all fall victim to overbooking from time to time.

Whether you use To-Do lists, day planners, electronic schedulers, or throw darts at a dartboard marked with client names, whatever plan you use to schedule your day needs to have a healthy dose of reality. A sure sign you've fallen victim to overbooking is when you *consistently* move projects from day to day. If half your To-Do list moves from Monday, to Tuesday, to . . . all the way to Friday, you're trying to do too much in one day—or you're procrastinating (covered in the very next section!).

When planning your day, it's wise to be ambitious. Erica consistently aims high. Her planner is chock full, but she knows if she never has to go to "Plan B," operates on all cylinders, and isn't interrupted by too many phone calls, she can "nail" her list. Does this happen every day? No, but that's why they call it life. Ambition is fine. Insanity is not.

Look at your list and ask yourself, if all the stars and planets are in alignment, if you never go to Plan B, and all of the rest of it, can you really achieve the list? If the answer is no, it's time to rein in your schedule. Why? For one thing, you may find yourself making promises to clients and sales calls you can't keep. You may miss deadlines; you may fail to return the calls you need to and so on. For another, overbooking builds into it a sense of failure. "I didn't do everything I planned to do." It may also, looking at a too-full schedule, induce anxiety, or make you feel under the gun constantly. It's not good for your psyche. Type-A personalities may thrive on this, but use caution for both your health and your sanity.

Procrastination: We Saved It for Last

We saved the ultimate Home Office Enemy—procrastination—for last. We even procrastinated about writing on this topic!

One of the toughest things about the solitary nature of the home office is procrastination. In an outside office, we all become attuned to working at a pace with our co-workers. We have people supervising us. We have an overall idea of how much work we are expected to accomplish each day. Working from home is solitary. Not only that, there are a thousand distractions. Joyce Lapsley, a Virginia-based consultant and trainer, says this about working from home: "Distractions/guilt about laundry, dust, etc. is one of the toughest things about working from home; that is, when I walk past a pile of dishes or laundry, I nag myself about them. On the other hand, when I'm relaxing, I feel that I should be working upstairs in the office." The problem with these distractions is they can often lead us to procrastinate on our work. While an on-site office has "busy work" or time-wasters, too, like water cooler conversations or personal e-mails, home offers other enticements, especially, for lack of a better word, "puttering" around the house. (You putterers know who you are . . .)

Home office procrastination, therefore, can be divided into two primary categories:

1. Lack of self-direction or motivation
2. Distractions of home

Let's tackle each of these in turn.

If self-direction is your problem and you find being alone leaves you daydreaming, not focusing, or not knowing where to turn first for a task, consider buddying up with another home office worker with a similar problem. In this new era of the home office revolution, there are *millions* of us out there. You probably know a few. Ask them if they would mind pairing up to conquer the procrastination bug. It might help to check in with someone as you would with a boss as you learn to motivate yourself, rather than having a supervisor choose the course of your day. You may even be able to do this online (see our website resources at the back of this book).

Another strategy might be to set off an alarm on your watch or an egg-timer for every 30 minutes, more or less. Chronic procrastinators can learn to value precious minutes by making them more measurable in terms of work accomplished. For instance, if you set your watch alarm to beep every 20 minutes, and it goes off and you realize you have spent the entire 20 minutes forwarding jokes on the Internet, surfing your favorite website, or daydreaming, you suddenly have a more vivid understanding of what happened in those 20 minutes—nothing! This can help train you to accomplish more by learning to set expectations for yourself for each block of time.

Motivational tapes help some people, as does music that "gets you going." Other strategies include mind games with yourself—or with the procrastination monster. First, you must figure out what you do when you procrastinate. In other words, if you like to make phone calls and gab with a friend for 10 minutes (or more) or you like to get up and snack (our own editor says this was one of his problems), set this up as a reward for a set period of time of solid working or the accomplishment of a dreaded task, such as filing.

Another technique is to figure out what particular office jobs you dislike the most in your home office. Do these tasks in limited intervals. Ten minutes of filing once a day is better than three hours of built-up filing at the end of two weeks. Commit to doing your least-favored tasks once a day, and don't give yourself mental permission to leave the office until you do.

A logical option is to pay someone to do those tasks you consistently procrastinate on to the detriment of your business. Can a bookkeeper do these functions once a week? What about a college student who can file or set appointments? See the box on "How Much Is Your Time Worth?" to determine whether this is a wise approach. Don't forget that just as you are telecommuting or setting up a home-based business, there are literally millions of others out there doing the same. Therefore, though you may hate to do your bookkeeping paperwork, you can bet the last dollar in your checking account that someone in your town or city is a bookkeeper who works from home by the hour. You may even be able to barter services.

How Much Is Your Time Worth?

When dealing with procrastination, it pays, literally, to know how much you are making per hour. Whether a telecommuter or home-based entrepreneur, you make an average hourly figure. Calculate that. Next, look at your most hated home office tasks: Filing? Bookkeeping? Appointment setting? Faxing and correspondence? Errands? Next, try to estimate what procrastinating costs you. In other words, if you put off correspondence until you have 30 letters to do, how long does it take to accomplish that—calculating a rough estimate of how much time you spent delaying, and doing other things to avoid the pile of letters (e.g., calling friends, visiting the refrigerator, etc.). Now calculate how much actual time it costs to do those letters. Not what it should cost, but what it's really costing your bottom line. In other words, if you make $50 an hour, and between wasting time over it, plus the actual chore of it, filing "costs" you five hours of time a week, that's $250. Now get pricing on how much it would cost to have this chore done by someone else. Finally, imagine your week free of this task and how much money you could make if you had extra time to place sales calls, do high-billing tasks, and so forth. Does it now make sense to pay someone to do your least-favorite work details? You may be losing money by doing them yourself!

What about people who get caught up in cleaning the house, laundry, mowing the lawn, or tinkering on the car? Technically, they're not really procrastinating, because they're getting actual household work done, but oftentimes, when examined closely, people who "putter" may actually be avoiding a work task they dislike. If this is you, then designate physical household chores as a way to combat mental tiredness. In other words, you are not allowed to use peak mental performance time to do a load of laundry or fix the leaky faucet. If you're truly mentally fatigued, use that time to do a chore, but also use it to stretch, take deep breaths, and increase energy levels. Even approaching chores as a way to invigorate, such as putting on your favorite rock 'n' roll as you fold laundry or clean the kitchen, or wearing a Walkman as you trim the hedges, can be a way to conquer procrastination in both your personal and professional life.

Again, it's all about playing mind games with yourself. And discipline. You're smart. You know your own pitfalls. Look at them and combat them in clever ways that bring you the end result you want.

There, procrastination wasn't all that bad, was it?

CHAPTER 5

ORGANIZATION: HOW TO GET YOUR ACT TOGETHER

The legendary blues singer Pearl Bailey once said, "I've been rich and I've been poor—rich is better." Well as far as we are concerned, we've been organized and we've been disorganized—organized is much, much better.

Organization is the nylon cord that holds both your home office and your home life together. It is pure chaos trying to run a home office without being organized. It's like trying to climb up a mountain of sand. Establishing a reliable system of organization under one roof is one of the most important acts of kindness you can do for yourself because a good system will change your life. Creating a dependable system is much easier than you may realize—and a whole lot faster.

So what does it take to make this amazing transition happen? We'd recommend that you change your mindset about who you are in this picture. You already are your own boss in a home office. Now it's time to imagine that you are also your own executive assistant. Every successful CEO has his or her own personal assistant working behind the scenes to ensure that everything runs smoothly. Each one of these assistants (many are well paid, by the way) has his or her own system of organization.

During our professional careers working from home offices, we each had embarrassing moments when we were caught being badly disorganized. Neither one of us had control over our home offices because there was no system in place. Yes, we both wanted to be our own CEOs but we neglected to also be executive assistants. As survivors of ineptitude, we can tell you that you do pay a high price for it. The lack of a sensible system of organization in your life will cost you in inconvenience, wasted time, lost dollars, stress, and embarrassment.

The Way We Were

Taking into consideration that we are asking you to take a hard look at bad habits, it is only fair that we fess up and share some of our more humiliating moments before we decided to get organized.

Kathy:

- A check worth $6,000 was lost in the house. It lay on the kitchen counter for a week before it disappeared. My husband and I turned the house upside down looking for it. Months later it was found inside a dog supply catalog in the laundry room.

- The water was turned off not once but twice because the water bills were buried deep in the back of a junk mail box. What's worse is that the bills had to be paid in person at a walk-up window.

- I never noticed the reminders sent in the mail that my Florida driver's license was expiring. As a result, I not only had to pay all kinds of fees, but I also had to retake the written part of the driver's exam. Talk about looking stupid and wasting valuable time.

Erica:

- I didn't file my taxes for three years. Uncle Sam was definitely not happy about this and gave me more than a quick smack on the head.

- At one point, I hadn't filed a single piece of paper, in either my personal files or business files, for one full year. I just had enormous heaps of mail, bills, and receipts stacked precariously high on top of my filing cabinets. Every time I looked at them, I got so ill, I couldn't make myself tackle the piles.

- I forgot a scheduled radio interview and literally was woken up by the phone ringing in my ear. The DJ was live when I answered the phone in a sleepy haze with no notes to refer to, along with two cocktails to my credit.

Without a system of organization in place, your home office and your family life will collide into one another like War of the Worlds. You'll go insane trying to juggle the two. A computer analyst for a large international company describes her lack of organization this way, "By Sunday night I feel like crying because I've gotten nothing done."

The desire to become organized has resulted in the birth of the professional organizer. The National Association of Professional Organizers, a professional organization of consultants, trainers, speakers, and manufacturers of organizing products, has more than doubled their membership since 1985. For fees ranging from $40 to $200 an hour, a professional organizer will come to your business or home to organize your closets or home office, and even assist with tag sales. Keep in mind that we're all not good at everything. Sometimes you need to call in an experienced person to guide you. Another option, one Erica utilized, is to ask a friend who is a wizard about organization to spend a day getting your house and office in shape. Reciprocate with dinner or helping your friend with something you're good at. Another option? Visit the "Fly Lady" on the Internet at www.flylady.net. She'll send you multiple organizational reminders via e-mail each day. Do each suggestion and voila—you're organized!

How Organized Are You (Really)?

Take the following quiz to see just how well organized you are. Once again, complete this quiz in the spirit of wanting to make some needed upgrades in your life. If you find that you score well, then bravo, you're in better shape than you imagined. If you find that you don't score well, take notice of the areas in need of improvement.

- Are you good at making up daily To-Do lists but not so good at following them?

    ❏ Yes   ❏ No

- Do you keep trying to build an exercise regimen into your day but never do?

    ❏ Yes   ❏ No

- Does the thought of getting your taxes together make the hair stand up on your neck?

    ❏ Yes   ❏ No

- Do your mornings feel chaotic and rushed as you're trying to get everybody out on time?

    ❏ Yes   ❏ No

- Do you have shopping bags or boxes filled with mail that needs to be sorted?

    ❏ Yes   ❏ No

- Do you constantly feel like you don't have enough time to get through your day?

    ❏ Yes   ❏ No

- Do you have to search for last year's tax returns?

  ❏ Yes   ❏ No

- Do the piles on your desk migrate from corner to corner until you finally get around to going through them?

  ❏ Yes   ❏ No

- Do you frequently pay your bills late because you have to sort through a pile of mail to find them?

  ❏ Yes   ❏ No

- Has it been longer than a year since you last purged your business files?

  ❏ Yes   ❏ No

- Do you write work phone numbers and messages on any handy scrap of paper?

  ❏ Yes   ❏ No

- Do you have to search the house for your keys, cell phone, or glasses more than once a week?

  ❏ Yes   ❏ No

- When asked for your Employer Identification Number (EIN), do you have to search through your files and paperwork before you find it?

  ❏ Yes   ❏ No

- When someone asks you to call him or her back, does it often take a few days just to find the time?

  ❏ Yes   ❏ No

- Do you sometimes have to plead your way into a professional conference because you missed the deadline to send them your check?

  ❏ Yes   ❏ No

- Would it be typical for you to let expiration dates lapse on your license, car registration, or insurances?

  ❏ Yes   ❏ No

- Do you sometimes have to send payments via an overnight service to avoid cancellations and late fees?

  ❏ Yes   ❏ No

- Do you get calls from creditors for late payments?

  ❏ Yes   ❏ No

- Do you constantly feel rushed when trying to make a business deadline?

  ❏ Yes ❏ No

- Do you keep planning to set up important things like a retirement account or college fund for your children but never get to it?

  ❏ Yes ❏ No

Did you get a perfect score and answer "no" to every question? Look us straight in the eyes and say that. If you are like the rest of us, you probably answered "yes" to four or more questions. Not to worry. You knew from the start that you had work to do on your organization skills anyway. Many of us secretly wish that we were more organized in our daily lives. How many times have you said to yourself, "Tomorrow, I am going to . . ."? The difference between those who are organized and those who are not is a choice. If you have made up your mind that you are going to be organized, then you are already on your way to a more productive daily routine.

Building a System of Organization in Five Quick Steps

An organization system is only good if (a) it's easy to follow and (b) it makes you feel like you are in charge of your life. There is no right system for everyone. In fact, you can create a system for organizing your life and your home office that is unique to you and your needs. You can keep it simple and follow the organization system mapped out in this chapter. If you are interested in more detail then peruse the Internet or your local library and you will uncover a million methods for becoming organized. You are free to choose one of these systems or pick the elements from a variety and customize them to meet your specifications.

All organization systems, no matter how flashy, have the same basic components. First, there is the physical plan for putting an organization system in place. Second, there is the action plan that you will follow daily. The key to becoming an organized person, or at least striving to be one, is trying to incorporate these elements into your daily life.

Step 1: Setting Up Your World (Location, Location, Location)

Every household should have a command center where all billing takes place, records are kept, and files are stored. If you work from home then the logical place for a command center would be around your work center.

Look around your home and decide where you would be most comfortable. A spare bedroom is perfect. You can also consider the basement or an attic room. A separate room puts a little distance between you and your family and provides peace and quiet. It's also easier to spread out. A few experts say to "never" put your office in your bedroom. That's fine, but what if that's all the space you have? A home office should be your nest and the place you feel you can get work done. If you are an author, editor, or telecommuter, then a home office in the bedroom should be okay. If you operate a small business and need to meet with clients or customers regularly then an office in your bedroom might be awkward. In those situations, consider holding meetings in your kitchen, dining room, or some other agreed-upon location (refer to Chapter 2 on the home office space).

Everything you need, from files to the fax machine, should be within your reach in a home office. It is a waste of time to have a filing cabinet in one room, supplies in a closet down the hall, and the computer somewhere else. There will be enough interruptions without you jumping up from your desk every five minutes to get something.

Step 2: Setting Up Your Files for Your Home Office and Your Home

A smooth-running home office goes hand-in-hand with a smooth-running household. Ignoring one guarantees trouble for the other. If you are going to take the time to organize home office files, then take a little more time to do the same for your household.

You will need:

- Filing cabinet: You can purchase a sturdy one at any office supply store. Don't go cheap and buy something flimsy because it won't last, the drawers will stick, and it won't be sturdy. Select a cabinet that holds legal size folders because some documents such as legal forms are longer than the standard 8 1/2 x 11 size.

- Hanging folders: Buy two boxes of legal size hanging folders in two different colors. Hanging folders can be bought in quantities of 25 or more and come in a variety of colors. Choose one color for your household and another for your home office.

- File folders: Buy two boxes of legal size file folders. Like hanging folders they can be bought in a variety of colors and can be purchased in quantities of 100 or more.

- One box of clear plastic tabs because the colored tabs can be difficult to read.
- One legal size cardboard filing box to be used as an archive for storing files at the end of the year.

Before you set up your files, make a list of what files you will need for your home and for your office. For example:

Home Files

Pick one color for your personal hanging folders. You should only need to set up the hanging folders one time. Some files fill quickly so you may want to set up several folders for the same heading.

For example:

Hanging Folders–Bank Statements: January–April,

May–August,

September–December

Use your file folders inside all the hanging folders. Label the file folders clearly so that you find them quickly. When the year is completed, all you will need to do is pull the file folders out, place them in your archive box, and start over.

For example:

Hanging Folder–Car

File Folders–Loan payments

Registration

Maintenance and repairs

The following are a list of possible file names for a family filing system:

Accounting–tax information

Banking–savings, checking account statements January to June, July to December

Car–insurance, repairs and maintenance, registrations, licenses, tickets

Charities

Credit Cards–listed separately

General Receipts—for general purchases such as clothes, toys, household items

House Maintenance—cable, landscaping, water, heat, electric

House/Renters' Insurance

House Receipts—repairs, appliance purchases

Legal

Life Insurance/Disability Insurance

Loans

Manuals—fax machine, printer, answering machine, VCR, television

Medical/Health Insurance

Pets—veterinary records, certifications

School Records—report cards, health records

Special Occasions—Christmas card list, gift ideas, gift receipts

Investments—pension plans, mutual funds, bonds, stocks

Telephone—house phone, cell phone

Travel and Entertainment—airline tickets, hotel and restaurant receipts

Warranties—for household appliances, etc.

Home Office Files

The following is a brief list of possible file names for a home business:

Accounting—tax information

Banking—savings, checking, statements

Bills/Invoices—paid and to be paid

Cable Modem (if available and necessary to your business)

Charities

Client and Customer List

Contracts

Credit Cards—used exclusively for your business

Insurance—keep a separate file for type of insurance (business, property and liability, etc.)

Legal

Loans

Office Supplies

Orders–pending, shipped, and canceled

Postal and Shipping Receipts

Professional–licenses, memberships fees, conferences

Telephone–business line, fax line, Internet line or DSL if no cable modem, cell phone, beeper

Travel and Entertainment

Tickler Folder–Keep this file for great ideas or projects you might like to develop later

A Catastrophe File for Your Family and Your Home Office

Nobody likes to think about tragedy, but in reality bad things do happen to good people. Nobody plans to die or become injured or ill. This file is important for your family and your business because it explains what your wants and wishes are in the event of your death or if you cannot speak for yourself. If you don't feel comfortable with this sensitive information in your home then leave instructions within the Catastrophe File explaining where it can be found. Is the information with your lawyer, a trusted friend, or in a safe deposit box? Your instructions might contain this information regarding your home and business:

Safe deposit box	Name and address of the bank; where the safe deposit key can be found.
Will	Where your will can be found; the executor of your estate.
Legal Guardians	An unsettling subject that many, many parents overlook. In the event of your death, who will be responsible to raise your children? This question is not easily answered, but you wouldn't want that decision to be in somebody else's hands. Choose that person, couple, or family carefully and make sure that they agree to be legal guardians for your children before tragedy strikes.
Living Will	Keep a living will in the event that you are unable to communicate your wishes regarding medical decisions.
Health Care Proxy	
Durable Power of Attorney	
Lawyer	Name, address, and phone number
Accountant	Name, address, and phone number
Insurance Policies	Name, telephone, and policy numbers
Bank Accounts	Bank names with account numbers

Credit Cards	Names and account numbers
Other Assets	Properties, investments, bills of sale(s) for major assets such as cars, homes, boats, art, jewelry, furniture, office equipment, and so forth
Outstanding Debts	Names, addresses, and account numbers
Key Contacts	List the names and telephone numbers of the key contacts involved with your business

Step 3: Coming Face to Face with Your Finances

Hold on a minute. Don't skip lightly over this section because it makes you feel uneasy. The idea of taking a look at the way we handle bookkeeping gives many of us the shivers. That knot in your stomach is fear. Fear can be a powerful, negative force that keeps you from doing the things you must do like getting a handle on your bills. Some people are afraid that what they find out will hurt them. The reality is that not having control over your finances always hurts more. Ask yourself this question: How can I know where I am headed with my finances if I don't have a map? Push the fear monster aside and take charge of your life.

You will need a record-keeping system for your finances. Keep your business financial accounts separate from your personal accounts. Maintaining separate bookkeeping for your home office is needed not only for tax purposes but also for accuracy. Remember that your goal is to keep your bookkeeping simple and easy to maintain. There are record-keeping options to consider such as using a software program or a handwritten record book. Software programs such as *Quicken*^{TM} and *QuickBooks*^{TM} by Intuit, *VersaCheck*^{TM} *Pro* by MIPS, *Peachtree Complete Accounting*^{TM} by Peachtree, or *Microsoft Money*^{TM} are examples of user-friendly programs that keep your business finances on track by tracking your finances, organizing budgets, bookkeeping, producing reports, charting profit and loss, and even printing checks. Ask your accountant, if you have one (and you should), for suggestions about picking the best software program for you. The IRS doesn't care how you do your bookkeeping as long as you are accurate, truthful, and can prove what you claim.

When running any business, it is important to know how you are doing financially. In other words, are you operating in the black or (gulp) in the red? How does your monthly income compare to what you are spending? Do you know where you make a profit and where you lose money? Is your business operating according to your business plan? Accurate and clear financial information provides you with a vital weapon to fight that fear monster.

An organized system for your finances saves you time and money. During tax season, you will be able to provide your accountant with all the information he or she requests. Each time your accountant has to call you to ask for this or clarification for that, you are wasting time and building up a larger bill.

> **Write this down...**
>
> *Avoid the last-minute scramble and keep all your tax information together in one place. We recommend using a folder or large, 9" x 17" envelopes. Clearly label the outside, (e.g., "Taxes 2003"). Inside, place a copy of your filed tax return plus your check stubs, receipts, and relevant documents. If you are ever audited, you will have everything all together in one place.*

Step 4: Setting Up Your Home Office Life

Who wouldn't agree that our lives are jammed with busy schedules and obligations? A system of organization used every day can make order out of chaos. Utilize the suggestions in this chapter and throughout the book as your guideposts. Daily routines save you time, keep you organized, and open the door for a fulfilling home life. What's more, you will be in charge.

Digging Through Disaster

One of the first steps in becoming an organized person is to purge and sort your current "filing system" of mail, bills, and documents. It is easier to become organized and stay that way once you rid yourself of paperwork and junk mail you no longer need.

Purge and sort the mail as soon as it comes in the door. Toss out what you don't want and don't need. Put the bills in a To-Be-Paid box, place the things you need to read in a To-Be-Read box, and file everything else. This simple routine takes only minutes a day and will save you a lot of aggravation later.

Eighty percent of what we save never gets looked at again.

If you are sick to tears by all the junk mail that clogs your mailbox, there is a way to put an end to it. The reason you may be receiving more junk mail than ever is because your name and address is being sold to others by direct-marketing agencies. Did you ever notice that when you order something by catalog you receive three or four new catalogs the next month? You can request your name be taken off the list by contacting:

The Direct Marketing Association
Mail Preference Service
P.O. Box 9008
Farmingdale, NY 11735
Web address: www.the-dma.org

> **Easy Steps to Handle
> Your Business Mail**
>
> - *Step 1: Sort your business mail from the family mail as soon as you bring it into the house. Separate the junk mail from your bills and papers you will need to file or read.*
> - *Step 2: Toss the junk mail directly into the garbage and be done with it.*
> - *Step 3: File all bills into the To-Be-Paid file.*
> - *Step 4: Open what needs to be filed; toss out whatever is not important, such as advertisements; and file directly into your filing system.*
> - *Step 5: Place the paperwork that needs to be read into a To-Be-Read box on your desk or create a To-Be-Read file.*
> - *Step 6: Set aside time one day during the week for paying bills and going through the To-Be-Read box.*

In Chapter 4, we discussed the benefits of keeping a day planner system for time management. A day planning system can be as simple as a notebook or a wall calendar. Office superstores such as Office Depot and Staples sell a variety of day planning systems such as *Day-Timer®*, *DayRunner®*, or *At-A-Glance®*. These systems can be bought for under $30 and come in a variety of sizes, themes, and colors. For those who prefer a more sophisticated planner, there are electronic organizers such as *Day-Timer® Electronic Page Organizer* for under $30 or, for more bells and whistles, the *Palm™ m105 Handheld Organizer* priced at about $150. The Palm organizers completely replace paper-based organizers and can also provide access to the Internet.

A day planning system can act not only as a great time manager but will enable you to be organized as well. Sit down and plan to fill in as many dates, appointments, and obligations as you possibly can. In fact, do the entire year in one sitting. As daunting as that may sound, it really can be done quickly.

For those who prefer the paper-based system (day planners, lists, calendars, and notebooks), using colored pencils or pens can be a fun way to keep track of your schedule. Keep separate what is professional from what is family. For example:

Red pencil:

Make this your home office color. Fill in all your meetings, conference calls, and deadlines.

Blue pencil:

Make this your children's color and write in all their after-school activities such as dance class, basketball games, performances, recitals, school events, parties, and even play dates.

Orange pencil:

Make this your family's color and write in all their birthdays, anniversaries, and family gatherings.

Green pencil:

Write in vacations, visitors coming into town, and day trips.

Purple pencil:

Make this your personal color. Think about scheduling all your recurring appointments for the year such as haircuts. Don't forget to schedule a little something extra for yourself—massage, yoga, daily walks, coffee with a friend, golf, or an afternoon at the park. If you don't put in something for yourself, chances are you'll put yourself last every time.

As simple as it may sound, using colored pencils in your daily planning helps you to see important appointments faster. On a busy day, your eyes will catch the meeting with a new client if it is written in red because it will jump out at you. Is it a bother to keep these silly pencils around? Many of the office superstores sell small boxes of colored pencils that are no bulkier than a hand calculator. Tuck them in the pocket of your planner, briefcase, or desk.

> *Instead of writing down phone numbers and important reminders on scraps of paper and the backs of envelopes, write everything down in one steno notebook or in a day planner. Don't forget to include the date!*

Step 5: Setting Your Work Week in Motion

A week can start off on the right foot or hit the skids as soon as the alarm sounds on Monday morning. The difference is being prepared for the week and knowing exactly what you want to accomplish. Your family and home obligations can take over your work time in a nanosecond if you don't prepare ahead of time.

Sunday Night: This is a good night to look over the week, decide what has to be done, and write your To-Do list for your work and for the household. We suggest not waiting until Monday morning to plan your week because if something unexpected arises, you'll be chasing yourself all day to get your list done.

The Night Before: Step 1: Get in the habit of preparing everything you will need for work and the household the night before. Clear your desk and lay out the work you plan to do first. If you have children, then their backpacks and lunches should be together on the kitchen counter or at the door.

Step 2: Get in the habit of laying out everyone's clothes the night before—don't forget your own. If you do this often, your kids will surprise you by laying out their clothes without you. Now that's one less thing you'll need to do! For many, getting fully dressed in the home office, rather than wearing PJs or sweatpants, helps them feel the most productive.

Step 3: Gather the mail that needs to go to the post office, deposits for the bank, and rental videos to be returned and sit it all next to your keys, sunglasses, cell phone, and To-Do list.

Good Mornings: Get up before the crowd and take care of yourself first. Do the things you like to do such as taking a shower, reading the paper, and getting dressed without interruptions. Once the gang is up and about, you'll be lucky if there are five minutes left for yourself.

Invasion of the Little People in Your Home Office

When you work from a home office and you have children, you have to face the fact that children will find every opportunity to be around you. Kids can find a million and one ways to interrupt telephone conversations or distract you when you are trying to beat a deadline. It is a fact of life. While your children may seem like little devils, in actuality they just want to be a part of whatever you're doing.

Try as they might, kids cannot resist their parents' desk with all those drawers overflowing with your cool stuff. Favorite pens are irresistible treasures disappearing faster than Halloween candy. Postage stamps, especially the expensive ones meant for bigger parcels, become sought-after "stickers" turning up on books, walls, and stuffed animals. In the minds' eye of a child, what's theirs is theirs and what's yours is theirs.

Don't rip your hair out—you can get a handle on this. Children feel better when they have a little structure and when they know what the rules are. If you have any doubt about this, watch how children play together and you will see that rules and consequences are a big part of their play. Times may

60 Seconds with Rhonda Levy

Rhonda works part-time from her home office handling medical billing and account receivables for her husband's podiatric practice. The flexibility of her schedule allows her to pursue her passion for tennis and to be very active in her children's lives. While she loves working from a home office and being available to her two children, it is sometimes a challenge to keep them out of her work and from touching her desk. Seeing the humor in it, Rhonda adds, "Threats and bribes do work wonders. I can only imagine when they're adults and how they might treat me when I'm around their important papers."

have changed, but children still love to play teacher or policeman. Listen and you will hear someone getting into trouble for breaking the rules.

Now that we all understand that children can wreck your desk faster than a pack of raccoons, here are a few quick suggestions to keep you sane:

Designate a Kid's Work Drawer

Kids love to pretend they are grown-ups. Pick a drawer in your desk or in your filing cabinet that is their drawer. It is a good idea to pick a low drawer that a child can reach safely and independently. Don't fill it with your children's things because that's not what they are after. Fill the drawer with the things you don't need anymore, such as:

Old stationery, envelopes, and business cards

Mailing stickers and labels

Out-of-service cell phones and beepers

Notepads

Plus, fill a shoebox filled with crayons, washable markers, and kid-proof scissors

 Write this down...

Filing cabinets can topple over if more than one drawer is open at a time. Never allow your child to stand in a drawer no matter how low to the floor it is. Consider anchoring it to the wall for the children's safety and in the event that you live in an earthquake region.

Designate a Sacred Drawer

This drawer is to be yours and yours alone. You are probably thinking that this is the one drawer your children will not be able to resist. There are a few options to choose from: You could put a lock on it or you could help your children to understand that this drawer is off-limits. If you let your children help to set up their own work drawer, they will be more inclined to respect your wishes about keeping away from your drawers. Be positive when you talk with your children about these special drawers. Reward them when they respect your wishes and stay out of your drawers. Tell them how proud you are of them when they listen. Remember, your children love you and want more than anything to be part of your world. It is possible to peacefully co-exist in your home office with children.

Your business will dictate what goes in your drawer, but some things to put there are:

Scissors

Tape

Stapler/staples

Favorite pens and markers

Ruler

Stationery, business cards

Blank CDs

Back-up files on CDs

Phone book

Cell phone

Checkbook

Rhythm of the Household

Households are curious places because they truly are a living, ever-changing system. It is not unlike a company with different departments and management levels. Introducing a home office into the system adds complexity (and chaos), but it can be done well. Achieving an organized household and home office takes just two steps: first, a plan is set in motion; second, the plan is followed. Maintaining an organized home and home office brings you one more step closer to your goal—success.

CHAPTER 6

PROFESSIONALISM IN THE HOME OFFICE

You Can Fool Some of the People Some of the Time

There's an old adage about "fooling" people. And the fact is that sometimes you can make your home office appear as professional and competitive as a large corporation. With professionally printed letterhead, a good phone system, proper business cards, a website, and so on, you can seem to the outside world as if you are actually working in a high and mighty corner office—when in fact you are operating from your dining room table.

For telecommuters, obviously people in your on-site office are going to know precisely where you are—at home! However, sometimes even telecommuters may want to seem to clients or potential clients on the other end of a phone call as if they are in a standard office. Perhaps it's the remaining bit of stigma that if you're working from home, you must be sitting at your computer in your bathrobe and talking on the telephone with one eye focused on the Jerry Springer show. Thankfully, corporations and others are moving away from the idea that working from home means you're wasting time, sitting around eating chips, or spending the morning perfecting your golf swing. Still, some people are reluctant to reveal they are a home office worker.

For people who are entrepreneurs, they may actually be competing with those in high-rise offices with a legion of assistants. Erica, for instance, wrote sporting goods radio commercials during the famous baseball "Subway Series," and she competed for the chance to write them against a large PR/advertising firm in the midwest. These types of competitive situations can make a home office person leery of letting people know they're at home. *Will I seem less professional?*, they wonder.

In addition to a fear of not being taken as seriously as a corporation in an office building, there is simply the reasonable ambition to seem as professional as one can be. After all, when pursuing business, if people are going to choose your budding company or you as a sales representative, and so forth, they are going to want to know that they are dealing with a professional in every sense of the word. And even more so if they are cutting you a big check!

Over time, Erica and Kathy have chosen to clue in some of those people we were "fooling" to the fact that we were at home. Some may have figured it out already. (Admittedly, if someone calls our homes close to the dinner hour, there's no mistaking the chorus of kids' voices and background chatter.) But the main point is whether you choose to let on that you are a home-based worker or company or not, you want to give off the air that you are a real pro. This chapter will tell you how to do that.

Letterhead, Business Cards, and Brochures: Make Them "Sing"

With the advent of laser printers, suddenly everyone believed they were a "desktop publisher." People could create everything from logos to postcards to mailing labels on their computer. They could buy software such as Print-master© and scores of other brands, or invest in a Macintosh® and graphics software, and even print out menus or brochures, color business cards, and so on. Four-color printers became affordable with ink-jet cartridges, and even laser printers came down in price.

While all of this desktop publishing could be seen as an exciting advent, it also ushered in some decidedly unprofessional work. For instance, Erica has been in publishing for 15 years. She has worked as an editor with best-selling authors. She knows how to spot a typo or poor grammar. Not everyone has this talent or skill. Therefore, she has been places such as doctors' offices, restaurants, and small shops and picked up brochures *riddled* with mistakes. Considering that this literature is sending out the company's or doctor's image to the buying or service-seeking public, it doesn't reflect well to have the brochure popped out from desktop publishing software full of mistakes. Perhaps money was saved—but at what cost?

While people now know how to design logos and create letterhead, and programs like Microsoft Word© can even lead you step by step in their creation, if that letter is printed out on cheap copy paper, what does that say about corporate image?

Business cards are often the worst offenders. Office supply stores sell perforated business card sheets that can be fed into laser or ink-jet printers. Once they're printed, a person simply bends on the perforation lines and has business cards—with tell-tale little rough edges.

What are some hard and fast rules to follow to present a corporate image—while keeping costs low?

1. If you cannot afford to have professional letterhead and envelopes printed at a print shop, at least purchase good-quality paper. Never use copy paper to send a letter to a client.

2. If you are an entrepreneur, consider hiring a graphic designer to pull together a corporate image for you, including a logo, unless you have a background in art or design. Just as you may have a home-based business, many graphic artists and students do, too. They may be priced more reasonably than a large firm. Thus the cost can be surprisingly reasonable, especially considering it may be your image for many years to come. Another option is to visit a local university and see if the marketing department or graphics department might like to take on designing a logo and slogan as a student project.

3. Never, ever use perforated business cards printed out of your laser printer. They look sloppy. With websites like *www.businesscards.com*, there is no reason to do this. The cost is minimal—and if you are a home office professional who thinks "time is money," the finished cards are delivered to your door so you don't even have to leave the house to have them done. Avery now offers no-perf cards to put through your printer, and these do have a more polished appearance. However, if you plan on handing out a lot of cards as you get your business off and running, printing up 500 or more is relatively cheap, and websites like *www.businesscards.com* even offer you design help.

4. Brochures should also be printed on a nice stock of paper. Paper Direct is an excellent company that offers a variety of brochure paper you can run through your laser or inkjet printer. However, and this is important, if the last time you thought about dangling participles and parallel construction was high school or college, consider having a professional design your brochure. Again, just in our networking circle we know a number of home-based PR professionals who design and create brochures at very competitive prices.

5. If you decide to go to a printer for your letterhead, envelope, business card, and other needs, you can opt for thick paper and a beautiful logo and skip two or four colors as a way to skimp on costs in one area but get the best in another.

6. If you get your paper and card needs at a printer, keep an eye on quantities when you get low. "Rush jobs" are almost always significantly more expensive, and it's one expense that is completely avoidable.

7. Finally, when designing your business cards and letterhead, remember this image may stay with you for a while. Make whatever is created for you "sing." Let the paper, font, logo, and business card reflect the image you want to present to the world.

Websites: Hitching a Ride on the Information Superhighway

Dot.coms . . . remember them and the fury of investing surrounding them? They sent Wall Street spinning on its axis, but then a funny thing happened (or not so funny if you were investing in them) . . . many of them fell out of their orbit and came crashing to earth. What does this mean for the home-based business?

In general, if you think simply putting up a website with products on the information superhighway is going to let you retire early, you may have to re-think that plan. On the other side, we firmly believe most or all businesses require a "presence" on the World Wide Web. Without one, you may seem woefully behind the times.

But what if, for instance, you're a one-person PR firm? You haven't many clients, but those you do have provide fairly steady work. You're savvy enough about how the Internet works to know that you don't expect to gather many new clients by simply putting out your shingle on the Web. Agreed. But, when going to meet a new client, we guarantee you one of their first questions will be, "Do you have a website I can check out?" Such is our culture now.

The first step, then, in pulling together a website, is to get your domain name. You may be frustrated and disappointed to find out your actual corporate name is "taken." You may then have to designate some variation of your name as your website. For instance, if your corporate name is:

Top Ideas, Inc.

You may find that:

topideas.com

is taken. Now what? Start playing around with your corporate name with things like:

topideasinc.com

topideasweb.com

top-ideas.com

One problem is that the farther you get away from your original name, the harder it is for people to find you. Another problem may be alternate spellings. For instance, if your company name is:

Two Girls Typing

Will people look for:

Twogirlstyping.com

or

2girlstyping.com

It pays, if you plan on using your website to drum up some kind of business, and if they're available, to buy the alternates and direct people who go there to your proper website. If you plan on doing something in the public eye, you might also consider buying the "negatives," such as:

Cartoonman.com

and

Cartoonmansucks.com

This is likely, as we said, only relevant if you do something in the public eye where this might spring up from a grudge or a competitor.

Once you buy your site through Veri-sign or any of the domain-registration companies out there (found on the Web), you'll need a hosting company that will allow you to "park" there until you get your website up. This book cannot possibly cover every bit of information about the Internet. That's another whole book entirely! However, the general idea is to get a hosting package that is competitive (no, they're not all priced the same). You must also decide how big your website is going to be and what its content will be. If you are going to have a "shopping cart" for people to buy products, much as you yourself may do when you visit a clothing shop on-line or Amazon.com, for instance, you need much more "space" than if you merely want two pages that tells a bit about you and your company. These are sometimes called "premium" packages, as they "reserve" more space for you than a site that is basically functioning as a "brochure" on-line.

Though the "shopping carts" for large companies are often designed with very intensive software, do-it-yourself versions are available. Therefore, you need to have some idea of the purpose of your website. Is it for advertising and corporate image purposes only or will you actually allow people to buy a product through it? Will you want to receive e-mail and get feedback from customers? Create a database from customer surveys, and so on?

What about design? Some amazing "do-it-yourself" kits are available that walk you through the process if you are pretty savvy. Jessica Stasinos, a publishing professional and indexer, designed her website by herself and hired a consultant for one hour to "load" it onto the Internet when that single process was just a little beyond her expertise. She is savvy on computers, and can load programs and download images. She is not a designer, but the software made it easy.

Erica herself makes no claim to computer genius. All sites related to her latest book releases are designed by web professionals she hires (all right, she married one). It's all in how comfortable you are on the computer, and where you want to spend your budget as you set up your home-based business.

Finally, once you have a website, remember that your image is out there on the Internet for all to see. If you make changes in your company, add new services, or have new credentials, remember to update from time to time.

Hold the Line: Phones in the Home Office

We covered phones in our technology chapter, but some of that bears repeating, at least in part.

When working from home, ideally your business should have a separate line. But often one line isn't enough. Erica's home has four. And depending on your business, you may follow suit. You might conceivably need a fax line, a line for your Internet provider, one line for your personal use, and one or more for business use. Besides keeping the phone company wealthy, what else should you consider when setting up phone lines for a home office?

- Regardless of how you do it (call waiting or an internal voice mail system that "bounces" clients or business associates into a voice mailbox), never have a caller for business reach a busy signal.
- If you spend a significant portion of your business day on e-mail or the Internet, have a separate line for that use.
- If household noise is a problem, return calls later rather than speaking to a client with kids crying in the background or your dog howling at the mail carrier.
- Just as when you are in a corporate environment, you are encouraged to have your day reflected on your voice mail, do so in your

home office. For example, "You have reached the voice mail of Joe Smith. Today is Monday, October 1st. I am at a conference until noon. Please leave a message, and I will return your call as soon as possible."

- "Cute" messages with music, silly sayings, or inspirational words are annoying to busy people. Leave a brief message for callers that allows them to speak as soon as possible.

- If your household has a number of people using the telephone (e.g., two parents and three teens), consider voice mail packages from the phone company that allow you to press different mailbox numbers.

E-Mail Etiquette: Minding Your Manners on the Internet

Most people picking up this book are familiar with e-mail. However, if we accept that this is the case, it's fairly amazing how many people aren't aware of the "rules of the road" when it comes to the Information Superhighway. Every week Erica and Kathy receive e-mails from people who clearly don't know professional e-mail etiquette. We don't mean to sound like Internet "Miss Manners," but there are a number of little rules to keep in mind when sending professional e-mail, so let's take a look at them.

- Never send an e-mail without doing a spell check. Only sending a sentence or two? Positive those two sentences have no errors? Guess again. You know this is true—you must get those e-mails, too. So do us all a favor and spell check.

- Keep humor or sarcasm to a bare minimum. Although something may seem funny or helpful to you, if read in a different light it may actually come across as inappropriately sarcastic, condescending, or rude. If you aren't sure about slang or abbreviations like IMHO (in my humble opinion) or LOL (laughing out loud)—DON'T USE THEM!

- In light of the previous comment, remember that the Internet is a culture. Do you know what flaming is? This occurs when someone posts a message to a news group or bulletin board and unintentionally aggravates other users, who may then send "flaming," rude e-mails back. In this culture then, abbreviations, slang, and comments in general can be perceived differently from when you speak them. It's there in black and white, yet it's open to interpretation. In person, someone might ask, "What did you mean by _____?" Clarification is readily available.

Not so in e-mail. Offend once, and you may even lose a client. At the very least, you may hurt feelings or alienate a budding relationship.

- Don't forward jokes and chain letters to professional acquaintances unless your relationship has expanded into a personal friendship—and ask if they mind getting jokes. Most professionals are simply too busy to wade through a lot of jokes. In addition, some companies have very strict policies about personal e-mail, offensive jokes, and materials. "Big Brother" is out there in many companies, so be wary.

- Just because it's the more casual format of e-mail doesn't mean common business letter courtesy is no longer used. Sign off with a "Sincerely" or "Very Truly Yours," include a salutation, and so forth.

- All those little "smileys" [;-)] or other "emoticons," as they are called, allow you to express emotion. But in professional correspondence, they're not appropriate. Let your words speak for themselves. And let those words be appropriate.

- If you want a colleague to look at a website, learn how to insert the link into your message.

- If you forward something that has already been forwarded a hundred times with "greater than" >> symbols galore or odd spacing, do your receiver a favor and cut, paste, and clean it up, particularly if it's very relevant to your client or associate.

- DON'T "SHOUT" IN E-MAIL. DON'T USE ALL CAPS.

- It goes without saying (but we'll say it anyway), off-color humor, sexist jokes, and even things as blatantly ridiculous as downloaded soft porn images that you think are funny to pass along will come back to haunt you. The rule of thumb many use is: If this was viewed by my boss or was saved by the person I sent it to, would I someday regret sending this (particularly if taken out of context)?

E-mail is a wonderful tool. It's fun at times. It cuts down on phone tag. It is all of those things. But it also can be used very sloppily. Don't be someone who doesn't follow the basic "rules of the road."

So there you have it. You may be one person at a kitchen table, but there's no reason you can't seem like a professional in every sense of the word! Follow these basic suggestions, and you're on your way to building a professional image of which you can be proud.

Nine Ways to Seem Bigger than You Really Are

Whether you are a one-person start-up or a sales rep trying to convey a professional image, here are a few ways to seem bigger than you are:

1. Use professionally printed letterhead and business cards.

2. Have a mission statement or a slogan that conveys your corporate image—just like the big guns.

3. If it's important for some reason to not seem like you work from home (if, e.g., you are in an industry where you routinely compete against very large firms), get a P. O. box. Also get one if you rent an apartment and/or move every year or two. It saves your clients from constantly having to note address changes.

4. Don't get caught answering the phone fresh out of the shower or with children crying in the background. Let voice mail be your friend.

5. Make sure all correspondence has been proofed and spell-checked.

6. Don't let your 12-year-old design your website (unless he or she is a junior Bill Gates). Let your Web presence reflect your image.

7. A professional image will only carry you so far. Back it up by never missing deadlines, not burning bridges, and meeting clients dressed to impress just as if you were in a corporate environment.

8. No busy signals—ever. No exceptions.

9. Don't let kids or anyone else answer your business line.

CHAPTER 7

GET THE BALL ROLLING: BUSINESS AND BUDGET PLANS

It is exciting to realize that the dream in your head could really come true—starting your very own company. If this is where you are at this moment then it is time to take the next step. The next step is to make yourself "legit" by deciding on your legal structure and constructing a business plan.

If you are serious about starting a home-based business, no matter how small or simple, you will want to set it up correctly from the beginning. Playing catch-up later on will cost you time, money, or even your business. Putting your business together with a well-thought-out plan can make the difference between success and failure.

The business plan is where you break your idea down into its important components. How are you going to manage, finance, and market this business? Have you worked out a realistic budget? What *is* a realistic budget? Getting all this information down in black and white will show you if you are ready to take the leap or if you require more time to plan and organize your idea. This would be a great time to seek out others in the same business for advice. Some may even be open enough to tell you where they made their mistakes. Believe us, it is much cheaper to learn from someone else's mistakes then your own. Once you have worked out a business plan, it's time to decide on a legal structure. In the next section we will go step-by-step through the various kinds of legal structures.

Start-up Options

When starting a home-based business, one of the first decisions to make is your legal structure. Now that you are going to open a home business, it is time to decide if you are going to be a sole proprietorship, partnership, or corporation.

Why should you incorporate? There are two important reasons to incorporate your business: the first is for protection against liability, and the second is taxes. Personal liability means that you are personally responsible for any debts or lawsuits involving your company. Your legal structure will determine how many taxes you will have and the schedule for payments. If you are not certain which legal structure is the right one, be wise and consult with an accountant or a lawyer for advice.

There are four legal structures your business may be structured as: sole proprietorship, partnership, corporation, and limited liability company.

1. Sole Proprietorship:

- Covers most small businesses and is the most common
- Easiest and least costly to manage
- One person owns and operates a business

Pros

- The owner has absolute control
- All profits belong to the owner
- The business can be terminated quickly

Cons

- Not having an "Inc." after your name could be a disadvantage when competing with other businesses
- You are on your own with no one to consult with
- It is more difficult to obtain financing should you need it
- The owner is personally responsible for all debts and liabilities involving the business
- The owner's personal assets are not protected from a lawsuit
- In the event of your death, the business dies with you

2. Partnerships

There are two types of partnerships: (a) general and (b) limited.

General Partnership

- A partnership means that you own and operate a business with a partner or partners
- Each partner has the authority to operate the business, hire employees, and handle the finances
- Legal fees are more than for a sole proprietor and less than incorporating

- A lawyer should be contacted to draw up a partnership agreement
- Partnerships should buy partnership insurance (see Chapter 10)

Limited Partnership

- This type of partnership has both general and limited partners
- The general partners run and manage the company
- The limited partners or silent partners act as investors and have no say in the operation of the business
- Limited partnerships do not face the same liabilities as the general partners
- This type of partnership has a lot of a paperwork and filing to look after

Pros

- Partners can supply more start-up capital
- Partners share in the management and the wealth
- Your profits are taxed as personal income
- You can pool your resources, talents, and energy
- Partnerships are relatively easy to set up

Cons

- The "divorce rate" among partnerships is higher than the divorce rate among marriages
- Partners are personally liable for any debts and lawsuits—even those brought on by their partners
- Partnerships can be difficult to dissolve. Dissolving a partnership can be acrimonious and result in lost friendships. The more detailed your partnership agreement is the less likely it is that this will happen.

3. **Corporation**

There are two types of corporations: C-Corporation, or standard corporation, and S-Corporation. The terms C-Corp or S-Corp refer to the way in which the corporation is taxed.

C-Corporation

- Standard for all publicly-held corporations

- Most complex of all business structures
- The cost of filing papers of incorporation through a lawyer can range from $300 to $1500
- Your business is recognized as a separate legal entity from you
- Corporations use "Inc." or "Corp." after their business name
- Corporations are required to issue stock, file annual reports, and elect corporate officers (e.g., president, vice president, secretary, treasurer)

Pros

- A corporation limits the personal liability of its owners
- The corporation's debt is not considered your debt
- Corporations can raise money, if needed, by selling stock
- Corporations live on even after an owner dies, retires, or sells

Cons

- Corporations are more expensive to set-up, run, and manage, require more attention from your lawyer and accountant
- Corporations are formed under the laws of the state in which they were created and are subject to that state's regulations
- Corporate owners can pay a double tax on the company's earnings (corporate and personal tax)

S-Corporation

- Also known as a Subchapter S-Corporation
- This type of business structure is popular with small business owners and entrepreneurs
- An S-Corporation is a pass-through entity, which means that there is no corporate-level income tax

Pros

- Permits the owners to avoid being double taxed by allowing shareholders to offset personal income with business losses
- Personal assets are protected from lawsuits

Cons

- Requires a substantial amount of paperwork
- Like a standard corporation, an S-Corporation must file articles of incorporation, issue stock certificates, hold shareholders meetings, and keep track of minutes at a meeting

4. Limited Liability Company (LLC)

- A mix of a partnership and a corporation; however, it is *not* a corporation
- Created to provide a business owner with greater liability protection without the double taxation (corporate and personal) of a corporation
- Liability is limited to the amount of an individual's personal investment in the company
- Owners are referred to as members rather than shareholders or stockholders

Pros

- Unlike an S-Corporation, which limits the number of stockholders to 75, an LLC has no limitation
- Provides the business members protection from any personal liability beyond what they invested in the company
- Capital can be raised through the limited sale of stock
- It is easier to obtain financing from lending institutions
- Unlike a limited partnership that prevents limited partners from having a say in the company, an LLC structure allows all members to participate
- Allows for pass-through taxation

Cons

- The regulations for LLCs can vary from state to state
- Just like partnerships and sole proprietorships, LLCs do not go on forever and may dissolve when a business member dies, retires, or becomes disabled
- If your company is going to do business outside of the state you live in, you will need to check the regulations for LLCs in other states
- There is a significant amount of paperwork involved

Getting the Paperwork Right the First Time

There are legal documents that need to be completed no matter which business structure you choose in order to operate your business. Getting them right will eliminate a lot of headaches and money later. You can be sure of that. The following is a list of the necessary documents for each of the business structures:

Sole Proprietorship	DBA Filing
Corporation (C or Standard)	Articles of Incorporation
	Bylaws
	Organizational Board Resolutions
	Stock Certificates
	Stock Ledger
S Corporation	Articles of Incorporation
	Bylaws
	Organizational Board Resolutions
	Stock Certificates
	Stock Ledger
Partnership (General)	General Partnership Agreement
Partnership (Limited)	Limited Partnership Agreement
	Limited Partnership Certificate
Limited Liability Company (LLC)	Articles of Organization
	Operating Agreement

Commonly Asked Questions Regarding Articles of Incorporation

Do You Need a Lawyer to Become Incorporated?

No. There are incorporation kits available that enable you to file and incorporate without the aid of a lawyer. There are software programs and Internet sites for incorporation. The advantage here is that incorporating yourself can save you hundreds of dollars. The disadvantage is that missing an important detail could cost you money and aggravation later on. We recommend that you do take the time to find a reputable corporate lawyer who can guide and advise you as your business grows.

What Are the Articles of Incorporation?

The Articles of Incorporation provide the information that is required by your state to do business. In general, this information includes the proposed name of the corporation, purpose of the corporation, names and addresses of the shareholders, and location of the corporation.

What Are the Corporate Bylaws?

Corporate bylaws are created by the corporation and describe how the corporation will run. The bylaws make clear what the responsibilities of the shareholders, corporate officers, and board of directors will be. Bylaws are for the corporation's use and do not have to be filed with the state.

What Is a Shareholder?

Shareholders have a financial stake in the corporation. They paid for stock the corporation uses for capital to run the business. Shareholders elect the board of directors for your corporation. Typically, when starting out new and small, the shareholders are those individuals who have created the business.

What Is the Board of Directors?

The board of directors is elected by the shareholders to set company policy, decide how the business will be run, and appoint the chief executive officers. What if you are in business by yourself? If you are alone then you are the only shareholder of the company. Therefore, as a shareholder you could appoint yourself as president, vice president, and treasurer. The only exception would be if your state requires that different people hold those positions.

What Are Shares of Stocks?

Shares of stocks represent a percentage of ownership in a corporation.

Are There Yearly Responsibilities
I Should Be Aware of?

First, make sure you file your tax return on time each year. Second, renew and pay your corporation fee when your state sends the renewal form. Miss this deadline and you will pay a stiff late fee. In addition, if you miss the renewal deadline within your state you will be considered unincorporated. Are you starting to see the domino effect developing? If you are now unincorporated you will have file for reinstatement and that costs time and money. If these details are not corrected by tax season you run the risk of running into trouble with the IRS. For example, you cannot file taxes as an S-Corporation (or anything else) if your articles of incorporation are null and void.

Your Business Plan

The road is littered with people who got very excited about creating a home business but never developed a plan to carry it out. More than a few thought, "I just want to open a little business from my house." The success of any business idea, no matter how grand or how small, depends on planning.

Most small home businesses don't call for elaborate business plans. A lengthy and detailed plan is needed if you decide to seek financing from third-party lenders such as banks, investors, or venture capitalists. Realistically, they want to know how viable the company is before they lend you money or invest in it.

Think of a business plan as your map for the journey you are about to go on. This map will direct you through places you have never traveled be-

Write this down...

For free step-by-step instructions on writing a business plan, visit the SBA website at www.sbaonline.sba.gov/starting/indexsteps

fore, such as marketing, financing, and managing a new business. Don't assume that you know the way on a road you have never traveled.

Basically, a business plan is composed of four parts: The components are: (a) description of your business, (b) marketing plan, (c) financial plan, and (d) management plan.

Why you should write one:

1. Helps to clarify what it is you want to do and exactly how you plan to do it.
2. Creates a map for you to follow and refer to as you go along.
3. Provides the necessary information should you seek third-party financing from a bank or investors.
4. Helps you to project your business into the future.
5. Makes clear how you will market, finance, and manage your new business.
6. Highlights who your customers are and where they can be found.

(1) Description of Your Business:
Keep these questions in mind when writing a description of your business:
- What is it you plan to do?
- What is your product?
- What is your intended legal structure?
- How will this product benefit your customer?
- Where will you run this business, and how much space will you need?
- Will you need storage; if so, how much and where?

(2) Marketing Plan:
When putting together a marketing plan for your company, consider some of the following questions:
- How do you plan to market this new business?
- Who are your customers? How old are they? Where are they? What sex? Income level? Education level?
- Do you know what your customers like and dislike? Do you know what they expect?
- How will you attract and hold this market?
- Who is your competition? Where are they?
- How is your competitor's business going? What are they doing right? Wrong?
- How is your competitor's product or service different from yours?
- How will you price your product or fees for services?
- How do you plan to advertise your product or services?
- What portion of your budget will be designated for advertising and promotions?

(3) Financial Plan:
This is a major component to any business plan because it takes money to make money. You should be able to answer the following questions:
- How much money do you have?
- Who will maintain your financial records and how will they be kept?
- How much money do you need to open your business? (Start-up Costs)

- How much money do you need to keep your business open? (Operating Budget)
- What is your monthly operating budget for the first year?
- What is your break-even point?
- How long will it take for your business to be profitable?

(4) Management Plan:

Let these questions help you as you write a management plan:

- How are you going to run this business from day to day?
- Will you run this business alone or will you have partners, employees, or both?
- How does your background, education, and experience prepare you for this new venture?
- What are your strengths and weaknesses?
- What are the qualifications of the people who will be working around you?
- What is your job description and responsibilities?
- What are the job descriptions and responsibilities of the people who will be working with you and for you?
- What are the hours of this business? Salaries? Vacation schedule? Benefits, if any?

Three Ways to Write a Business Plan

There are three ways to write a business plan depending upon your budget and the complexity of your new business venture. The individual who plans to teach silk flower arrangements from home needs a simple plan while the person beginning with investment capital or bank loans requires a more detailed plan.

- Free: The SBA provides a wealth of free information and help for writing business plans, including planning templates and advice. In addition, there are many business websites such as *About.com* or *Entrepreneur.com* that can direct you to free downloadable business plan templates. *Invest-Tech.com* and *BizPlanIt.com* are two other sites that not only sell software programs but also provide free sample business templates.

- Under $100: There are several good software programs on the market for writing business plans. *Business Plan Pro®* by PaloAlto.com is currently the best-selling business plan software program on the market.
- Over $1000: If you are forming a company that includes significant investment start-up capital and a complex legal structure, you may want the help of a business planning consultant. These are professionals who will write the plan for you, charging anywhere from $1500 to $5000. They can be located on the Internet, in the yellow pages, or from your accountant.

Giving Your Business a Name

Deciding what to name your business can be fun, but it is also important and needs to be carefully thought out. A clever business name attracts customers and is easy to remember. It should represent you and what you do. If your business name does not include your name (e.g., Susie Smith), a "doing business as" or "dba" name will have to be filed with the county clerk in most states unless it is a corporation.

- A business name shouldn't box you in. The name should allow you to expand and grow.
  Example: Children's clothing
  > Good name: Amanda's Closet
  > Bad name: Amanda's Sleepwear
- A good business name should make sense to others and not just to you
  Example: Editorial business
  > Good name: WriteStuff
  > Bad Name: Opus Lexicographer
- People should be able to pronounce your business name easily. If they can't pronounce it, they sure aren't going to remember it.
  Example: Silk flower arrangements
  > Good Name: Forever Fresh
  > Bad Name: Ersatz Arrangements

When you decide on a business name, conduct a screening search to see if anybody else is already using it. If you go ahead and use a name that is registered by someone else, they can seek legal action against you. After all, would you like it if somebody were using your business name? Your accountant, lawyer, or local business office can tell you how to do a business name search in your area. Do a national name search if you plan to do business outside the state you live in.

Can't come up with a clever business name? Why not throw a business naming party? Invite your family, friends, and other business people to vote on the names they think are the best. If you've tried and tried but just can't think of what to call your new business, there are companies that will develop and research a name for you. Shop around because prices can vary.

Employer Identification Number (EIN)

EIN identifies your business for tax purposes, the same way that a social security number identifies you as a taxpayer.

You will need an EIN if you:

- Plan to form a business other than a sole proprietorship
- Plan to hire employees for your business
- Need to withhold income tax
- Plan to fill out payroll reports
- Plan to pay taxes
- Plan to open a business checking account

A sole proprietorship does not always require an EIN because if you work alone you are not an employee of your own company. In this case, you would use your social security number to identify yourself when filing your taxes. However, if you are a sole proprietorship with employees, you need an EIN.

You may file for an EIN by completing Form SS-4. These forms can be found on the IRS website or at your local post office or library.

Registering a Website

Now that you have decided on a business name and registered it with your state, you may want to think about securing a website name and creating a website. Even if you don't think you want a website right now, you may want one later. Securing a website name is still inexpensive and will be available if you need it.

On the Internet, a website name is referred to as your domain name. Your domain name starts with "www" and ends with either ".com," .net," or ".org." To register a domain name for a business website, you will need to register the name with an accredited registrar. For a listing of accredited registrars, visit the InterNic website at *www.internic.net*.

Why you should consider a website for your business:

- With more and more people going on-line, a website can be an important advertising tool.
- Websites are accessible to your customers or clients 24 hours a day.
- Unlike a magazine ad or brochure, a website can be updated or changed as often as you want.

Disaster Plans for Your Business

It is difficult to think about disaster when you feel so good about starting your own business. But in life, bad things can and do happen. Mother Nature has been known to make more than her fair share of disasters. Her wrath can take many forms, such as floods, tornadoes, hurricanes, earthquakes, ice storms, blizzards, and flash fires. Of course, there are also the man-made kind of disasters, such as house fires and theft.

Keep a copy of your licenses, permits, tax information, incorporation documents, and contracts someplace outside your business, perhaps in storage at a warehouse or in a safe deposit box.

Get into the habit of backing up your files and keeping those discs in a safe place such as in a safe deposit box. Don't forget to routinely back up your website because hosting companies can crash. If your mailing list is in your website and there's a crash, a valuable business resource will be lost.

When it comes to insurance, make sure you have enough. Sure, there are the obvious losses such as office equipment and inventory, but what about the less obvious—your salary, equipment leases, and loan repayments? Contact your homeowner's insurance company to find out exactly what they will and won't cover. A home office is not automatically covered just because it's in your home. Does your homeowner's insurance cover business equipment? You can purchase additional insurance to cover the things not insured by your present policy.

Keep a file of emergency contacts off-site in the event your home office is destroyed. This file should contain names, business addresses, e-mail addresses, account numbers, and policy numbers for the following:

Accountant

Banking

Clients or customers

Credit cards

Distributors

Federal emergency numbers

Insurance

Lawyer

Office equipment—make and model, receipts, serial numbers

Purveyors

Suppliers

Checklist for Success

While starting your own business is exciting, it seems like there are a million details to take care of before you can get started. As you scan down this checklist, you may see items that don't pertain to you. Businesses can differ in structure, size, and complexity. Use the following checklist as a guide to keep you on track for success.

❑ Write your business plan and include details for marketing, financing, and management

❑ Budget your start-up and operating costs

❑ Decide what legal business structure best fits your home-based business (sole proprietorship, partnership, corporation, limited liability company)

❑ File the required forms for your business structure

❑ Decide on your business name

❑ Conduct a search for your business name to make sure no one else is already using it

❑ Register your business name

❑ Obtain the appropriate business licenses and permits

❑ Check what zoning restrictions, if any, exist in your town or community

❏ Register or reserve state or federal trademark

❏ Register copyright

❏ Apply for a patent if you are selling something you invented

❏ Order a business line for your telephone number and fax or arrange for a second line on our home phone

❏ Conduct a search on the Internet to see if your business name is available for a website

❏ Once you have a website name, register it so that no one else may use that name

❏ Create your website

❏ Investigate what insurance you may need to obtain, such as property and liability, business, umbrella liability, business interruption, disability, health, life, and key man insurance for partners

❏ If you plan to have employees in your company you will need to file for an EIN

❏ If you are going to hire employees, contact the Department of Labor to see what laws relate to you

❏ Find out about workers' compensation if you are going to have employees

❏ Open a business account at your bank for checking and savings

❏ Once you have registered a business name and set up your legal structure, order your stationery and business cards

❏ Apply for a sales tax number if you will be selling a product from your home business

❏ Have your accountant or lawyer give you the necessary information about tax filing and record keeping

For the latest information on trends in home-based businesses and home franchises, we suggest you visit Entrepreneur *magazine's website at* www.entrepreneurmag.com.

❏ Make a list of supplies and equipment you will need to start your business

❏ Other

_____

❏ Other

_____

❏ Other

_____

❏ Opening Party!

Start-Up Costs Worksheet

Item	Cost	How You Will Pay
		(Cash, credit card, installment plan)

I. Equipment

1. Computer
2. Printer
3. Copier
4. Fax
5. Telephone
6. Answering machine

Subtotal: _____

II. Furniture

1. Desk
2. Chair
3. Filing cabinets
4. Bookshelves
5. Lighting
6. Desk accessories

Subtotal: _____

III. Telephone

1. Business/fax line
2. Installation charges
3. Listings in phone book

Subtotal: _____

IV. Website

1. Website design
2. Securing and registering a website
3. Monitoring the website

Subtotal: _____

V. Office Supplies

1. Stationery and business cards
2. Hanging and file folders
3. Binders
4. Mailing envelopes

                                        Subtotal: _____

VI. Licensing and Permits

1. Business license
2. Seller's permit
3. Fire certificate
4. Zoning permits
5. State occupational license

                                          Subtotal: _____

VII. Advertising

1. Promotional materials
2. Ad space
3. Media

                                          Subtotal: _____

Other Important Costs

1. Postage and shipping
2. Insurance
3. Benefits
4. Loan payments
5. Dues and memberships
6. Legal fees
7. Accounting fees
8. Storage
9. Start-up inventory
10. Replacement inventory

11. Entertainment and travel
12. Your salary
13. Other salaries
14. Fees from credit card processing
15. Fees from other sources such as e-commerce

Subtotal: _____

Total: _____

What you estimate your first year of income to be from this business:

_____

What you estimate your first year of expenses will be: _____

Other monies you have available, if necessary: _____

(Other paychecks, savings accounts, stocks, life insurance, properties, gifts)

Have Map, Will Travel

Deciding on and choosing a business structure along with writing a business plan takes a lot of time, energy, and discipline. But every minute spent on developing a clear, well-thought-out plan will come back to you in spades. A business plan isn't like the history report you did for Mr. Campbell back in high school, when you wrote the report, got a grade, and tossed it into the back of your locker. A business plan is about you and how you plan to set a course to meet success in this new venture. We'd recommend that you keep it close by and refer to it often. A good business plan is going to show you if you're starting to veer off course. That's a red flag nobody wants to miss. Savvy business people suggest that a business plan be updated once a year to help fine-tune goals and plans. The better you understand your business plan, the better you understand your business.

CHAPTER **8**

TAXES: DON'T GET CAUGHT ASLEEP
AT THE WHEEL

Here we are at the one chapter that makes everyone uneasy and anxious. Taxes. Everyone has a good tax or IRS story, and we're certainly no exception. One of the authors of *The 60-Second Commute*, whose name shall go unmentioned (she's the tall one), still gets a little jittery around the tax "subject." Why do taxes stir up so much anxiety? First of all, tax codes are complex, and the forms could send you running for a Valium. If you're ever feeling particularly masochistic, visit the public library or go online to the IRS website and check out Forms and Publications. Your head will explode. Second, these folks at the IRS take accounting very seriously. On one occasion, Kathy had the opportunity to meet an IRS agent in a social setting. While she can't remember a thing the woman said, she will never forget seeing the size of the agent's badge.

Being afraid or nervous about taxes is a normal reaction, but that still doesn't let any of us off the hook. Grumble as we do, we all have to pay taxes to the federal, state, and local government.

In this chapter we are going to review many of the tax subjects that are important to running a home office whether you are in business for yourself or a telecommuter. Use this chapter as a reference to help get you started. Every business can be a little different from the next, so contact your accountant or tax advisor with specific questions before you get into trouble.

There are tax issues we must all get straight right from the beginning no matter what kind of tax filing we do. When it comes to taxes, there are deadlines and specific rules for filing. If taxes are paid late or not at all, there are financial penalties (usually with interest).

When it comes to taxes you should know:

- How much will you have to pay?
- When will you have to pay?

- What deductions can you take?
- How can you defer your taxes?

The complexity of your tax filing depends upon the type of work you do. If you are a telecommuter, tax filing is not as complicated or as daunting as it can be for a small business. A telecommuter or someone who works from home for another company might consider using one of the popular tax software programs currently available and file his or her own taxes. Currently, the best-selling tax preparation software in the country is *Intuit's Turbo Tax Deluxe*®, *Intuit's Turbo Tax*®, and *H&R Block's Financial Taxcut 2000 Deluxe*®. These are the best selling because they are the most user-friendly, offer tutorials, provide expert tax advice, and guide you through the return process. But we caution you that user-friendly does not mean "easy" and using these programs requires more than simply punching in the numbers. You will need some degree of knowledge to understand how these figures correlate to one another. Bear in mind that mistakes will cost you when it comes to the IRS.

Your Accountant

Some experts say that a small start-up business does not require the services of an accountant. The answer is—maybe. Before you attempt to handle your own taxes, answer this question: How good are you at handling your personal taxes? Do you prepare your own personal returns? Do you pay on time or ask for extensions? Have you ever been audited? This is really the litmus test. Filing business returns is more complex than personal returns.

If money is an issue (as it often is in new businesses), then try to learn as much as you can about your tax obligations before getting started. There are many places to turn for advice such as the Service Corps of Retired Executives (SCORE), a national organization sponsored by the SBA. SCORE volunteers are actually retired business executives who are happy to provide financial counseling and workshops—for free. You can find a SCORE office in your region by looking in the yellow pages of the telephone book. In addition to asking advice at SCORE, you can attend tax seminars for small businesses, do some research at the library and on the Internet, consult friends or other people in business, or buy computer software programs and books on the subject. There honestly is a lot of information out there.

Here's our advice to you: Unless you are well-versed in tax law, tax codes, home business deductions, and filing procedures and very responsible about staying on top of everything, then you are taking the risk of making mistakes by filing your own taxes. Mistakes will cost you time, aggravation, and potentially a lot of money lost in unclaimed deductions or in penalties because of filing errors.

Don't be cheap when investing in yourself and the success of your business. Be honest. Maybe you have good accounting skills, but are you prepared to stay on top of it? Are you knowledgeable and disciplined enough to know when to file certain tax forms, submit quarterly taxes, keep consistent financial records, and claim the right home business deductions? It can be a lot of information to stay on top of, especially when you're also managing and marketing a new business.

Your accountant needn't be from the biggest and flashiest firm in town to be competent. On the other hand, it also shouldn't be your cousin Lenny who's never done a business return in his life. A good accountant should have experience in handling small businesses. Ask those you trust or other small business owners who they use. Don't feel funny about asking an accountant for a few referral names. An accountant worth his or her salt should pass the information along willingly. If an accountant bristles at the suggestion of providing referrals then he or she is not right for you.

Accountants' fees vary depending on location and client base. For example, you can assume that the accountant in Beverly Hills with entertainers as clients is going to charge more than a local accountant in the suburbs. In general, accounting fees can range from $75 to $200 an hour or higher.

Once you've put your finances into the hands of a reputable accountant, don't for one minute think that you can stop paying attention. While accountants are knowledgeable about bookkeeping, the role of an accountant is not to be a bookkeeper. The primary job of an accountant is to analyze your financial records and prepare your tax returns. If you feel like maintaining your books from week-to-week and month-to-month will get away from you, then perhaps hiring a bookkeeper is an option.

Jumping Off Point

As we described in Chapter 7, all business owners must have a taxpayer identification number. The reason for this number is so that the IRS can identify you and process your tax returns. To review, there are two types of identification numbers: first, a Social Security Number (SSN) and second, an Employer Identification Number (EIN). SSNs are issued by the Social Security Administration and appear in a nine-digit form that looks like 000-00-0000. An EIN is issued by the IRS and also appears in a nine-digit format but looks like 00-0000000. All estimated tax payments for income tax of a sole proprietor must be recorded under the SSN.

When do you need an EIN:

- Whenever you have employees, even if you are registered as a sole proprietor
- If you operate as a corporation or partnership
- If you have a qualified retirement plan
- If you file returns for employment taxes; sales taxes; excise taxes; or tobacco, alcohol, or firearms taxes

How to get an EIN:
Complete Tax Form SS-4 (*Application for Employer Identification Number*). You may do this several ways:

- Fastest method: Fax—call (800) TAX-FORM
- Internet: *www.irs.ustreas.gov*
- Slowest method: Filing by mail will take from 4 to 5 weeks

When to apply for an EIN:

- You should apply for the number before filing your first business tax return or make a tax deposit. If you haven't received your EIN by filing time, send in your tax return anyway. Clearly write "Applied for" along with your application date in the EIN box on your tax form.

Deciding on Your Tax Year

When you begin a business, you will need to decide on what tax year to use. A tax year refers to the accounting period used for your financial records, reporting income and expenses, and filing to the IRS. This means that you are going to keep a set schedule for your books and taxes for the year.

There are two types of tax years:

- **Calendar Year**—If you choose a calendar year then you will need to begin bookkeeping on January 1st and finish on December 31st of each year. Most businesses choose the calendar year method because it is easier and parallels their personal income filing. If you are a sole proprietor, in business for yourself and by yourself, then the IRS requires that you file according to the calendar year.

- **Fiscal Year**—Like the calendar year, a fiscal year covers a 12-month period. You may end your fiscal year on the last day of any month except December. Remember that the last day in the calendar year is December. In other words, if you choose to start a tax year on March 1st, then according to the fiscal year system, your tax year will end on February 15th. In addition, special requirements apply to fiscal year requirements. The first year can always be a short calendar year.

 **Write this down...**

If you intend to change your tax year, contact the IRS by completing Form 1128. Naturally, there will be a fee.

Which Accounting Method Should You Use?

The IRS requires that a business use a consistent accounting method for keeping its books. By accounting method, the IRS is referring to a set of rules for deciding when and how to report income and expenses. The two most commonly used accounting methods are the cash method and the accrual method.

- **Cash Method**—The cash method is used most by individuals and small businesses. All income is taxable in the year it is received and all expenses are deductible when paid. There are a few exceptions when the cash method cannot be used.

    You may not use the cash method if (a) you are a partnership that has a corporation as a partner or (b) you produce, purchase, or sell merchandise and keep an inventory. In the case of the latter, you will need to use the accrual method.

    For example, a small publisher could not use the cash method because he or she would have books in inventory.

- **Accrual Method**—The reason for an accrual system of accounting is to match income and expenses in the current year. If your business has an inventory then you are required to use the accrual method of accounting. Taxes are paid on earned income even if you haven't received those payments. Expenses can be deducted as they occur, whether or not those expenses have been paid or not. In other words, your income is recorded when an invoice is sent out and expenses are recorded when the bill is received. With the accrual method, there are receivables, (e.g., the money that is owed to your business but not yet received), and payables, (e.g., the money you owe but have not yet paid). For instance, you created and sold holiday gift baskets during the holiday week of December 24 through 31. You use a calendar year accrual method of accounting. Although your customers pay in January of the new year, you would include the amount received as part of your last year's income.

Keeping It Simple

Certainly all this information can seem overwhelming when just starting out on a new venture. Talk about taking the wind out of your sails. One key way to stay coherent while handling taxes is to keep a consistent, commonsense approach for record keeping. Here are a few pointers:

- Keep track of your customers and orders by using prenumbered sales invoices. Without some kind of numerical system for your receipts, it is almost impossible to track sales.
- A business should have its own bank account. Mixing business accounts with personal accounts opens the door for mistakes and may attract the IRS' attention. That's attention no one needs—believe us on that.
- When a customer or client makes a payment, deposit it in full into your business bank account. At the end of the month you can determine your monthly income by comparing bank deposits with paid invoices.
- Pay all business expenses from your business bank account. If you don't, your accountant will have to take additional time to sort out business from personal transactions, which will result in possible late filing fees and a higher accounting bill.
- Money taken from your business that is not considered a salary is referred to as a draw. Keep track of this by maintaining a draw column in your ledger.
- Use your business check register as a cash payments register.

There are many good reasons to keep organized and consistent records for your business aside from saving time and aggravation. Well-maintained records provide information regarding profit and loss, expenses, cash flow, and most important, your bottom line.

Keep any and all records related to the running of your business. This includes payments made to your business, bills paid out, and all expenses. Save all your check stubs, deposit slips, invoices, and purchase orders. These items serve as your proof for the entries made into your bookkeeping ledger. For example, if you purchase a new laser printer for your home office and enter it into the books as a business expense, you should also have the receipt in case the IRS wants to see proof of purchase.

Taking a Look at Your Track Record

By now it's probably apparent that one of the reasons to maintain your financial books is so that you can see how you're doing in business. If you own a small business and either sell or produce products or provide a service to customers, you will want to know if you're making a profit, covering your expenses, or operating in the red or the black. The best way to see how you're doing is to create the following three statements:

- **Profit and Loss Statement (P&L)**—This statement is straightforward and to the point. A P&L shows your income or revenue and your expenses for a given period. If you do a monthly P&L, then you will be able to see your progress each month. These statements help you to compare one month, or quarter, or year to another.

- **Cash Flow Statement**—A cash flow statement analyzes the money that comes in versus the money that goes out. From the cash flow statement, you can project cash flow trends and determine if you will have enough money to pay your bills and operate your business. If you are a young business just starting out then having a cash flow projection will tell you whether or not you can cover expenses.

- **Balance Sheet**—A balance sheet shows you what your business is worth. It indicates the difference between your businesses' assets and liabilities. Assets would include cash, accounts receivable, inventory, and equipment. Liabilities would include such entities as your debts to creditors, loans to the bank, accounts payable, and income taxes.

Most home businesses don't have to do a complicated financial analysis to keep records straight. But there is an advantage in knowing your business' financial bottom line. What's the advantage? Financial reports tell you whether you are operating in the black or the red, whether you can spend or need to save, and whether or not you are traveling along the course you intended to follow.

Home Office Deductions

Running a home office means that you may be entitled to deductions above and beyond the typical business deductions. The advantage of a home office deduction, if you qualify, is that you can deduct part or all of your home that you use for business.

Unfortunately, some people make the assumption that if they have a home office or even if they work from home, they can create all kinds of tax deductions. That was true for a long time until the IRS got wise to it. People got greedy and abused the home office deduction by reporting everything from dog food to posh vacations to cosmetic surgery. There are those still pushing the envelope and they need to be careful. Sooner or later, the IRS becomes curious and starts snooping.

What Is a Home?

The IRS will consider your cozy domicile a home if it is one of the following:

- *Apartment*
- *Boat*
- *Condominium*
- *House*
- *Mobile Home*

If you ask the IRS, they will tell you that there are four criteria to meet in order to qualify for the home office deduction.

1. Exclusive Use

To qualify for Exclusive Use, there needs to be a specific area in your home that is used only for your business and nothing else. In other words, if you run a small catering business from your kitchen, you cannot qualify for Exclusive Use because you also use that kitchen to cook the family's meals. But if you had a separate kitchen, perhaps in your basement, used exclusively for your catering business, that would qualify.

There are, however, two exceptions to the IRS Exclusive Use guideline. The first refers to space used to store inventory or product samples. The second refers to the use of your home as a day care facility.

If you would like to claim inventory space in your home as a business deduction, you will need to meet the following five conditions:

- You are in the business of selling either wholesale or retail products
- The inventory you want to claim is for your business
- The only fixed location for your business is your home

- The inventory space is used on a regular basis
- Your inventory space (garage, basement, attic, shed, etc.) is suitable for storage and easily identified as storage space

Not sure if your storage space qualifies? Let's say you sell ladies' brow shavers in a mail order catalog from your home and you store the shavers in your garage. You also house your car in this space. The garage would be deductible even though it is not used exclusively for your business.

The IRS permits a home business deduction if you use your home on a regular basis as a day care facility. The IRS recognizes that a day care facility might be for children, mentally or physically challenged persons, or seniors over the age of 65. Before you can claim your home or part of your home as a day care facility, you must have applied for, been granted, or be exempt from having a license, certification, registration, or approval as a day care center or as a family or group day care home under state law. Obtaining a license means that your home will have to meet certain criteria for the safety and well-being of the children or adults in your home. Where can you find out about this business license? Visit or contact your local government office for the specific requirements in your area. A word of caution—operating a day care facility without a license is a violation, resulting in steep fines and liability if someone is hurt or injured while under your care.

2. Regular Use

To qualify for Regular Use, you need to use the specific area on a continuing basis. You don't meet the criterium if the area is used occasionally. However, some businesses are seasonal; that is, there are months when you are not in operation, such as landscapers and pool maintenance people. As long as the area designated for work is not used for anything else, it still can qualify for Regular Use.

3. Business Use

If you are actively operating your business from your home, you can meet this criterium.

4. Principle Place of Business

To meet the requirement for this criterium, your home office must either be your principle place of business or the place you routinely meet with clients and customers.

For instance, suppose you are in the business of art restoration and your work is conducted at estates, museums, and private homes. As long as you use your home office exclusively and regularly for your bookkeeping and administrative operations, then your office will qualify.

Perhaps you are a public relations consultant with an office across town. As long as you regularly meet with clients in your home, you can deduct your home office. Caution—your home office does not meet the criteria if it's used only to receive telephone calls or to hold occasional meetings.

Determining Your Partial Deductions

If you meet the aforementioned conditions, you will be able to claim your home office as a deduction. Now you will be able to claim deductions that are directly related to running any business, but you can list indirect expenses than can apply to your home. The IRS permits you to partially claim the following indirect expenses.

- Community or condominium association fees
- Homeowners insurance
- Housekeeping
- General repairs (i.e., air conditioning)
- Mortgage interest
- Real estate taxes
- Rent
- Security system
- Trash collection
- Utilities

How do you figure the amount of indirect expenses that you can claim under your home office deduction? With a formula, of course! It's not hard so don't get too jittery.

For the first step, you will need to determine the percentage of your home dedicated to your home office space. Use this formula:

Square Footage Method

$$\frac{\text{Office Square Footage}}{\text{Total Home Square Footage}} = \text{Business Percentage}$$

Example:
Suppose you run a freelance editorial business from a spare bedroom in your home. The size of your office is 10′ x 10′ or 100 square feet. The total square footage of your home is 3,000 feet.

$$\frac{100 \text{ sq. foot office}}{3,000 \text{ sq. foot home}} \ = \ 3 \text{ percent}$$

You can deduct 3 percent of your home's indirect expenses as a home office deduction. For instance, you can deduct 3 percent of your mortgage interest or 3 percent of your real estate taxes. Using IRS Form 8829 – *Expenses for Business Use of Your Home* (PDF), follow the list of step-by-step calculations to determine the amount you will be allowed to deduct. According to Form 8829, you are first permitted to deduct mortgage interest, real estate taxes, casualty losses, and anything that is carried over from the previous year. Then you can deduct such items as utilities, maintenance and repairs, trash removal, and security systems if you still show a profit. If you're fortunate enough to still be showing a profit, you can deduct the depreciation on your home office. We would like to stress that before deducting expenses under the home office rules, a thorough review and evaluation should be made of how it will relate to the exclusion of the gain on the sale of your primary residence.

Business Deductions

All businesses are entitled to a variety of deductions. The IRS says that an item or expense is deductible if it is "ordinary, necessary, and reasonable" for a business to run. The following is a list of possible business deductions that are good for the year in which the expense is incurred. For more information, we suggest you speak to your accountant, or tax advisor (both are tax deductible) or visit the IRS website.

Advertising giveaways (promotional items)

Advertising expenses

Answering service

Association and memberships dues

Automobile mileage

Bank charges

Beeper

Business cards

Business directories

Business gifts

Business insurance fees

Business telephone

Business trip expenses (hotel, food, transportation)

Cellular telephone

College courses

Commissions

Consultant fees

Copyright registration fee

Employee salaries

Equipment charges and repairs

Interest on business credit cards

Interest on business loans

Internet access and online service fees

Journals, periodicals, and books related to your business

Licenses and certification fees

Office furniture and equipment

Office maintenance and repairs

Office supplies

Payroll taxes

Postal and shipping charges

Postal supplies (boxes, labels, envelopes)

Professional fees (accountant, lawyer, bookkeeper)

Publicity and public relations charges

Seminars, workshops, and conferences

Start-up costs

Stationery

Training tapes

Tolls and parking fees

*Explanation of Typical Business Deductions
and Expenses*

While businesses are entitled to claim deductions on such expenses as auto-mobiles and entertainment, specific regulations must be met before the deduction can be claimed.

- **Automobile Expenses**—If you use your car, van, or truck for business, there are two ways to deduct business-use charges. The most popular is the mileage deduction. The IRS permits 34.5 cents per mile in 2001 and 36.5 cents per mile in 2002 for business travel in a given year. The second method is to itemize your automobile deductions: Use a depreciation deduction on the cost of your automobile and then add to that all of the costs related to running that vehicle, such as gas, oil, tires, repairs, parking and garage charges, tolls, insurance, and license and registration charges. The deduction will then be based on a percent of total business miles divided by total miles driven everywhere. No, no—the IRS won't let you deduct parking tickets so you had better keep plenty of parking meter change in your vehicle.

- **Education**—The IRS permits you to deduct education expenses as long as they are related to your business, trade, or occupation. The IRS states that to claim this deduction, the conference, workshop, seminar, or college course must either maintain or improve your skills or be a continuing education requirement for your profession (i.e., doctors, psychologists, realtors). Sorry—the IRS does not allow you to deduct education expenses if you are changing careers or starting a new business. In addition, courses to meet the minimum educational requirements for your education are not deductible (i.e., law or medical school).

- **Health Insurance**—You can deduct health insurance if you are self-employed. As it stands now, a self-employed individual may deduct 70 percent in 2002 and up to 100 percent in 2003. Add the remainder you can't deduct to your itemized medical expenses. If the amount of medical expenses is then over 7.5 percent of your gross income, the remaining medical expenses are deductible.

- **Retirement Plans**—A self-employed person can claim deductions made to retirement plans such as an Individual Retirement Account, Simplified Employee Pensions, and Keogh plans. Income earned from retirement plans is tax deferred. Contributions made may be tax deductible.

- **Entertainment**—The IRS allows a deduction of 50 percent on entertainment expenses if they are directly related to your business. The key is to keep good records documenting your business entertainment expenses. You can deduct restaurant charges, cocktails, and even theater tickets. When taking a client out for a meal, make sure to keep the receipt and record the date, time, place, and purpose for your meeting. Planning a business party? Along with the receipts for catering, flowers, and hired help, keep the guest list as part of your business documentation. Keep documentation explaining the reason for the dinner or party—just holding onto the receipts won't cut it.
- **Gifts**—The IRS allows you to make deductions for business gift giving. Gifts are deductible up to $25 per person per year.
- **Start-up Expenses**—If you are just beginning a new business, the IRS will permit you to deduct up to $25,000 in 2002 for start-up expenses such as business equipment, phone systems, computers, and fax machines. It is considered a first-year expense deduction. The alternative choice is to deduct the cost of the business equipment using IRS tax code depreciation schedules over a period of several years.

Erase These Items Off Your Deductions List

The IRS has gotten pretty clear about what business deductions you may and may not take. Tempting as it may be to add some of these items to your deduction list, you run the risk of alerting the IRS to an audit. You don't want to do that. The following is a list of deductions the IRS will not permit:

- Adoption
- Airline clubs
- Country clubs
- Divorce expenses (Exception: expenses associated with tax advice)
- Dog tags
- Funeral expenses
- Golf and athletic clubs
- Health spa
- Hotel clubs

- Illegal bribes and kickbacks
- Life insurance premiums
- Lunch with coworkers
- Marriage licenses
- The cost of using an entertainment facility (i.e., yachts, hunting lodges, fishing camps, swimming pools, vacation resorts)
- Parking tickets
- Personal disability insurance premiums
- Personal legal expenses
- Political contributions
- Wristwatches

Self-Employment Tax

If you work for yourself, even on a part-time basis, and earn an income from it, the IRS expects you to pay self-employment tax. What is self-employment tax? Self-employment tax is really two combined taxes—Social Security and Medicare. Recall that when you received pay stubs from previous employers there were deductions made from your check each week under a box called FICA (Federal Insurance Contributions Act). In that case, both you and your employer paid equally into your FICA. FICA consists of 6.2 percent Social Security tax and 1.45 percent Medicare tax.

When you work for yourself, you are expected to pay both the employer's share as well as the employee's share. With all these tax obligations, it's a wonder people start any businesses at all. But to lessen the blow, the IRS allows you to get a deduction for one half the FICA paid on the front of Form 1040. Form 1040 SE will complete the entire calculation.

Child Care Tax Credit

If you work from home and hire someone to care for your children, you are entitled to claim a portion of the cost as a child care tax credit. The amount you are permitted to claim as a tax credit is dependent upon your adjusted gross income. The amounts are capped at $2,400 for one child and $4,800 for two or more children. Both spouses must have earned income for this to apply unless filing as a single parent.

When to File Your Tax Return and What Forms to Use

In general, the due dates for filing your business tax returns are based on two key elements: the legal structure of your business and whether you use a calendar or fiscal year as your tax year.

1. **Sole Proprietorship**—If you are a sole proprietor, you will use these forms when completing your tax return:

   Schedule C—*Profit or Loss from Business*

   Form 1040—*Individual Income Tax Return*

   Schedule SE—*Self-Employment Tax*

   Form 8829—*Expenses for Business Use of Your Home*, if your home office qualifies

2. **Partnerships and limited liability companies**—If your business is structured as either a partnership or limited liability company, you will use these forms when filing your return:

   Form 1065—*U.S. Partnership Return of Income*

   Schedule K-1—*Partner's Shares of Income, Credits, Deductions*

   K-1s are distributed to the partners or the limited liability company members and are a required portion of the tax return. Like the sole proprietor, filing dates depend on the tax year you have chosen.

3. **Corporations**—If your business is structured as a corporation, you will use these forms when filing:

   Form 1120—*U.S. Corporation Income Tax Return*

   or

   Form 1120 S—*U.S Income Tax Return for an S-Corporation*, if you are structured as an S-Corporation

   Form 2553—first year only for S-Corporations

   Schedule *K-1*—*Partner's Shares of Income, Credits, Deductions*, if you are an S-Corporation

4. **Filing Dates for Corporations and S-Corporations**—For corporations using the calendar year, the due date for taxes is March 15. For corporations using the fiscal year, the return must be filed by the fifteenth day of the third month after the end of your corporation's tax year.

Who Pays Quarterly Taxes?

The IRS says that everyone who is self-employed has to pay quarterly taxes. Who is self-employed? You are, if you are a:

- Sole proprietor
- Partner in a partnership
- Member of a limited liability company
- Shareholder in an S-Corporation

The reason for quarterly taxes is because as a self-employed person, you don't have an employer withholding income tax from your paychecks each week. Therefore, you are expected to make payments based on your estimated federal income tax. These taxes are typically referred to as quarterly taxes because they are due on a quarterly schedule:

- April 15
- June 15
- September 15
- January 15

How do you make quarterly payments to the IRS? Use Form 1040-ES, which can be obtained by calling 800-TAX-FORM or by downloading it from the IRS website at *www.irs.gov*. After the first year, the IRS will send these forms to you automatically. If you are using any of the widely used software programs (i.e., *Intuit, Quicken, H&R Block*), all these forms can be printed from the program.

How do you know how much to pay? The important thing to remember is that you want to avoid underpayment penalties. Here's the guideline to follow for making estimated quarterly taxes:

- If your adjusted gross income is under $150,000, you will need to pay at least 100 percent of last year's tax liability. In other words, if you paid $5,000 in taxes last year, you will need to make quarterly payments of $1,250 this year.
- For the year 2002, if your adjusted gross income exceeds $150,000, then you must pay 112 percent of the amount you paid last year.

What if this is your first year in business? All first-timers should use last years' tax return as a way to figure your estimated tax payments.

Now that you have this all figured out, here's one more thing—you will probably be expected to pay state taxes. State taxes follow the same quarterly payment schedule.

An Independent Contractor or an Employee?

It is important as a business owner to correctly decide if someone is an employee or an independent contractor. There is a general rule for determining one from the other:

- **Independent Contractor**—According to the IRS, a person is considered an independent contractor if you, the business owner, have the right to control or direct only the result of the work and not the means and methods of accomplishing that work. A periodic bookkeeper is an example of an independent contractor because he or she was hired for a specific skill and required no training from you. Be smart and write out a simple agreement with an independent contractor that describes what he or she will do for you. Ask the contractor to provide you with invoices.

- **Employee**—According to the IRS, a person is considered an employee of your business if you can control what will be done and how it will be done. If someone is an employee then you will have to withhold income taxes, withhold and pay Social Security and Medicare taxes (FICA), pay unemployment tax on wages paid to the employee, and possibly other fringe benefits.

What can happen to a business owner if he or she incorrectly claims someone as an independent contractor instead of an employee? Unfortunately, the IRS expects you to make this determination correctly because if not then you can be held liable for back employment taxes for that person plus accrued interest and penalties. Determining the difference between the two can be confusing and expensive if you make a mistake. For instance, typically a lawyer is considered an independent contractor, but he or she can also be an employee. To sort this all out, the IRS provides specific guidelines in Publication 15-A (*Employer's Supplemental Tax Guide*).

The Important Month of January

Once the independent contractors have been sorted out from the employees, it is important to remember that January is an important month for mailing out tax forms. Who gets what and by when?

- **Independent Contractors**—IRS Form 1099 (*Miscellaneous Income*). An independent contractor should receive a Form 1099 if you have paid that individual at least $600 last year. Additionally, you will have to send out a Form 1099 to anyone who was paid over $600 in royalties, rent, prizes, or broker exchange transactions. Independent contractors should have their 1099s from you no later than January 31.

- **Employees**—An employee should receive IRS Form W-2 (*Wage and Tax Statement*). The W-2 form lists how much money the individual was paid and the amount of FICA, federal, and state taxes you withheld. Like the independent contractors, employees should have their W-2s no later than January 31. Form W-3 summarizes all W-2s prepared by the employer.

- **IRS**—The IRS will need Form 1096 as a cover page summary for all your Form 1099s.

- **Social Security Administration**—Remember to send them a copy of all your employees' W-2 forms.

- **Finally, don't forget**—Don't forget individual quarterly returns (i.e., Form 941 and state), as well as Form 940 for Unemployment Taxes

Where Can You Get These Forms?
There are four ways to get your hands on these precious forms:

1. Office supply stores sell packages of Form 1099s
2. Your accountant usually has extra forms
3. Telephone the IRS at 800-TAX-FORM and request that they be mailed to you
4. Stop by a local IRS office

Flying Below the Radar

Filing taxes may make you jittery, but nothing clears a room faster then a call from the IRS. Remember that classic scene from *The Honeymooners* when Ralph Cramden gets a call from the IRS instructing him to come down to their office right away? He nearly dies from fright only to find out it was nothing at all. Not to stir this pot up further, but did you ever see an IRS agent's badge? An IRS agent does indeed carry a big badge, and it makes a police badge look silly. Okay, maybe that was more information than you needed to know.

There are ways to keep the IRS away from your door, as well as ways to be prepared in the event that they do come calling. It is never too soon to keep organized and accurate records. Receipts are important but they are not enough; you should maintain a log book during the year.

The following may be obvious, but people make these mistakes all the time:

- File your tax returns—That may sound funny, but the self-employed represent the largest group of nonfilers in the country.
- Sign and date your returns—Your return is not considered complete without your John Hancock.
- Remember to put your SSN or your EIN on your returns.
- Pay any income tax that is due when you file.

The IRS knows that individuals and businesses have been abusing deduction claims for a long time. Deductions are definitely a flash point for the IRS. Here are a few that the IRS might red-flag:

- **Charitable contributions**—If your business makes a charitable contribution, then you should keep a record of your donations. Whenever you can, write a check for all your contributions. In the record, indicate the organization, date, and amount of the contribution. The IRS requires that all contributions over $250 include a written receipt from the organization. A fast and efficient way to keep this information handy is to set up a hanging folder in your filing system and label it Charitable Contributions. Keep a charitable log in the file, then each time you make a contribution, make a notation in the log, along with the letter or receipt into the file for safe keeping.
- **Home Office**—For years, people have been trying to write their house off as a home office deduction. But the IRS has very specific requirements for claiming this deduction. First of all, claim just the space that is actually your home office. Be sure that the percent ratio is correct before you submit the information in your tax return. If you claim repairs and utilities, then make sure to hold onto these receipts. Be really smart and take a photograph of your home office. Keep the photograph tucked away in a safe place in the event of not only an audit, but a fire, natural disaster, theft, or if you move.
- **Entertainment**—The IRS provides a clear list of what entertainment, travel, and dining deductions are acceptable. Get into the habit of keep-

ing concise records in an entertainment and travel log that makes clear the date, place, purpose, who was present, and amount. It is not enough to just keep stubs and receipts.

Do Sole Proprietors Run a Higher Risk of Being Audited by the IRS?

The word on the street is that this is the case. According to *Small Business Information* at *www.about.com*, sole proprietorships are more likely to be audited over partnerships, S-Corporations, and the general tax-paying population. Aside from glaring mistakes, omissions, and large deduction claims on a tax return, the IRS also considers income as a factor for an audit. One thing is certain—the more you make the greater your chance of being audited.

Commonly Asked Questions

- **Am I really supposed to report all the money I make?**
  Yes, every penny. No matter how you make money or how much, the IRS expects you to report your earnings and pay taxes on it.

- **How could the IRS know whether I report all the money I make?**
  Trust us—they have their ways. In fact, there are several ways the IRS could learn of your unreported income. First, suppose the IRS audits one of your customers. In that case, the IRS can elect to audit all the companies that do business with this company. Second, a 1099 form filed by another company or individual does not match your income. Third, a disgruntled client or partner could report you to the IRS just to harass you. The IRS will investigate their reports and may conduct an audit. Fourth, your return may attract attention because of either substantial losses or profits. Fifth, you may not know this but the IRS does conduct random audits and your name could be selected. Sixth, the IRS also looks at lifestyle and determines if reportable income can support it.

- **What happens if I don't file a tax return?**
  This wouldn't be a good habit to get into. Imagine a snowball rolling downhill and growing larger and larger. When you don't comply with the tax codes and regulations established by the IRS, there are penalties to pay. In the event that you don't turn in a return at all, you will be charged with penalties. The penalty is set up this way: 5 percent of the unpaid tax for each month or part of a month that the tax is unpaid. This 5 percent can jump to 25 percent or more of the tax depending on the circumstances.

What if you fail to pay the penalties? You could really be digging a hole for yourself because once again, there are penalties for that.

- **I sell handcrafted picture frames at house parties. Am I supposed to report this small income to the IRS?**
Yes, you will need to indicate this extra income on your tax return. Additionally, you may have to pay income tax and even self-employment tax on your profits. And keep this in mind—if you live in a state with sales tax, you ought to be collecting it with every picture frame you sell.

- **I am thinking of creating a part-time home business as a web designer. What taxes am I supposed to pay to the IRS?**
People who work for themselves are expected to pay the following: federal income tax and self-employment tax if you earn more than $400 for the year. Check with your accountant to see if you are also obligated to pay local and state income taxes.

- **How long should I keep my tax returns and tax-related records?**
If you want to rest easy, keep your tax returns forever. Think of it as your tax time capsule. Store them away in a safe place and if you ever need them, for whatever reason, there they are. This is also true for property records. Toss them in with the tax returns. All records related to your taxes, such as cancelled checks, receipts, and other tax documents that appear on your return, should be kept until the statute of limitations expires for the return. When is that? Typically, it is three years from the date the return was due or filed or two years from the date the tax was paid, whichever date is the latest.

- **What is a tax credit?**
A tax credit is not the same as a tax deduction. While a tax deduction entitles you to make a deduction off of your taxable income, a tax credit entitles you to take the credit amount off of your final tax liability. For example, if you owe $15,000 in taxes, you can subtract the tax credit directly off of this amount.

Tax Software
There are three tax preparation software programs that are flying off the shelves.

- *Intuit's Turbo Tax Deluxe*
- *Intuit's Turbo Tax*
- *H&R Block's Financial's Taxcut 2000 Deluxe*

Tax Guide Books

- *Taxes for Dummies.* Eric Tyson and David Silverman. Hungry Minds: Chicago, 2001. Paperback, $16.99.

- *H & R Block Income Tax Guide.* Simon & Schuster: New York, 2001. Paperback, $15.95.

- *J.K. Lasser's Taxes Made Easy for Your Home-Based Business: The Ultimate Handbook for Self-Employed Professionals, Consultants, and Freelancers.* Gary W. Carter. John Wiley & Sons: New York, 2000. Paperback, $16.95.

- *The Vest-Pocket CPA.* Nicky A. Dauber. Prentice-Hall: Upper Saddle River, NJ: 1997. $16.95.

IRS Publications

There may be plenty about the IRS that can make you nervous, but we recommend a visit to their website for a thorough compilation of reader-friendly publications. Whether you are a telecommuter, freelancer, or small business owner, the IRS has the tax information you seek. You can find these publications online at *www.irs.gov/formspubs/display.html* or by contacting the IRS at 800-829-1040.

Publication 334 – *Tax Guide for Small Business*

Publication 463 – *Travel, Entertainment, Gift, and Car Expenses*

Publication 529 – *Miscellaneous Deductions*

Publication 533 – *Self-Employment Tax*

Publication 535 – *Business Expenses*

Publication 538 – *Accounting Periods and Methods*

Publication 541 – *Partnerships*

Publication 542 – *Corporations*

Publication 547 – *Casualties, Disasters, and Thefts*

Publication 587 – *Business Use of Your Home (Including Use by Day Care Providers)*

Publication 15-A – *Employer's Supplemental Tax Guide*

CHAPTER 9

LEGAL EAGLES:
UNDERSTANDING YOUR BUSINESS AND THE LAW

It's like the character George Costanza used to say on *Seinfeld*, "Why must there always be a problem?" In the life of a home-based business, why must there be so many codes, regulations, guidelines, and laws? Oh, please. Like taxes, we could debate the subject of legal codes and requirements until we turned blue in the face. Some are necessary to keep us safe and out of danger while others provide revenue to federal, state, and local governments. Then of course, there are other laws and statutes no one can make sense of because they are outdated and otherwise inane.

---

60 Seconds with Brian McCarty

Brian McCarty is an expert juggler. Not a juggler in the traditional sense, he doesn't toss pins up in the air, but Brian almost always has several things going on at the same time. Brian works 12-hour shifts as a police officer on Long Island and is also the owner of CST Technologies, a computer consulting company that he operates from a home office. CST stands for Caitlin's School Tuition, and Caitlin is Brian's five-year-old daughter. As a single father, raising a child on his own can be a challenge—but one that is well worth it. As Brian puts it, "Everything I do, I do for my daughter. She is my focus. I work the night shift so that I can be available to Caitlin during the day. I've created CST Technologies because I want to be able to provide whatever she needs—whether it's a private school or step dancing." What's next for Brian? He wants to develop an import-export company.

In this chapter, we are going to address the legal issues that are typically associated with a home-based business, such as business licenses, permits, copyrights, and trademarks. But we're going to start off with a discussion about lawyers and the importance of not only having one, but also of picking the right one.

Hiring Your Lawyer

When you think of a lawyer, think of a long-term close relationship. Your lawyer is your confidant and someone you should be able to trust and rely upon. The lawyer you choose to work with should not only be a legal expert in your area of business, but he or she should also be interested in working with you. You need to know that when "push comes to shove," your lawyer is willing and able to represent you with the necessary skill and expertise.

To find the right lawyer for you begin by asking around and collecting a few reputable names from people you trust. It's important to remember that, like doctors, lawyers have specialties. Would you see an orthopedic surgeon for a heart condition? This same rule applies to lawyers. Would you use a personal injury attorney to handle your business contracts? Ask for recommendations from individuals or businesses in your industry. When you have collected three or four names, contact those lawyers for an interview. It is reasonable for you to expect that an initial interview or consultation with a lawyer is free. The following is a list of qualities your lawyer ought to demonstrate:

- Experience in your area of interest
- References of satisfied clients
- Empathy for your concerns
- Availability to you

You may be wondering why we didn't include reasonable fees in the list of important qualities. In our opinion, your comfort level with a lawyer's fees is personal and one that only you can answer. Typically, a lawyer's fees can range from $75 to $400 per hour. Lawyers' hourly fees depend, for the most part, on their specialty, their experience, size of their practice, and their location. Keep in mind that sometimes there is no positive correlation between fees and service—expensive doesn't indicate better. Once you have decided on your lawyer, expect he or she to draft a letter of engagement that will detail the nature of your relationship and the billing method. To keep your costs down, be prepared with the relevant information and paperwork whenever you meet. And remember—unlike your mother, you shouldn't call your lawyer 1,000 times a day because he or she *will* charge you. When you're talking to your lawyer the clock is always ticking—always.

The following is a true story about Kathy and her small publishing company:

While Kathy confesses to making several mistakes as a publisher, there were actually a few things she did right. When it came to picking a lawyer, she chose a lawyer who also represented some well-known publishers and successful authors. Despite the fact that Kathy was in south Florida and her lawyer was in New York, she decided to go with the best legal representation possible. She knew that small publishers face an uphill battle against the mighty larger publishers. Kathy chose an entertainment lawyer on Madison Avenue with 30 years experience, a long list of references, and an excellent reputation.

Early one spring morning, the telephone rang. It was the president of the national distributing company that was handling Kathy's line of books. He was upset and talking on his cell phone about Kathy stealing a cover from one of the largest publishers in the world. On the brink of a heart attack herself, Kathy listened as the president described getting a cryptic phone call from this publisher's legal team telling him that his "little" publisher had better change the cover of one of her books because it was the same one they were using. There was just one problem—Kathy's book had come out before the big publisher's. In fact, their cover came out after Kathy had placed a large color advertisement in *Publishers Weekly* to promote the book. The question really was who stole what from whom?

Kathy's head was spinning. She called her lawyer in New York immediately because she feared that this powerful publisher could actually force her to pull the book off the bookshelves. Kathy's publishing company would have taken quite a financial hit, to say nothing of the author's disappointment. Her lawyer laughed, "You've made my day. I love it when the big guys try to bully the little guys." He called the legal team representing the larger publishing company and said that he wanted to meet with them immediately.

The publisher's legal team didn't know who was coming, but they assumed that a publisher this small must have a lawyer who worked from the back of a station wagon. When Kathy's lawyer walked into the meeting, every member of the legal team knew who he was. Collectively, their jaws dropped to the floor. He then told them, "Gentlemen, I have a problem and I need your help. How can I convince my client to not sue you for stealing one of her covers? How do I stop her from leaking this to the *Wall Street Journal*?"

Kathy didn't want to sue anyone nor did she want to create any sensation in the media. She only wanted to get her author's books on the shelves. For her, picking the best lawyer possible was one of the smartest business moves she ever made. Her lawyer, in just one short visit, put an end to a situation that could have gone the wrong way in the hands of a less experienced attorney.

Making Sure You're in the Zone

One of the first steps to take when beginning any new business, whether in a home office or elsewhere, is to make sure your area is zoned for the type of business you plan to operate. Zoning regulations vary a great deal from place to place. For instance, did you know that in some parts of the country the zoning laws date back to the Civil War while in other parts of the country there are no restrictions at all? There are some places where operating a home office is not permitted.

Zoning laws are important and can be a good thing. They are one of the ways that your local government keeps residential areas residential, business areas business, industrial areas industrial, and agricultural areas agricultural. They are also intended to protect us from danger or unsafe situations. Consider the Black Mamba snake for a moment. The Black Mamba is considered to be one of the deadliest snakes in the world. Death from this 14-foot serpent can occur in less than 15 minutes if it bites you. Imagine for another moment that your next-door neighbor gets the bright idea of breeding these snakes from his or her home and selling them over the Internet. Without zoning laws in place, there would be little you could do to stop your neighbor from raising these lethal, slithering creatures. As a basic rule of thumb, there are regulations in place if somebody's business puts others at risk.

Typically, zoning laws are in place to control:

- The type of business you conduct
- Parking
- The amount of traffic in your area
- Using signs for advertising purposes
- The hours when your business may be in operation
- The use of hazardous materials and chemicals
- How many people you employ in your home business
- How much of your home is designated for your business
- How much odor, smoke, and noise your business will generate

It is important to remember that zoning laws can vary from town to town and county to county. What is permitted in one area may not be permitted in another. For instance, in Manhasset, New York, a realtor is not allowed to solicit potential home sellers by telephone, but in the very next town of Port Washington, it is permitted. How can you find out about the zoning laws in your area? Contact your local government agency and ask for the Zoning Department, Planning Department, or the Building Inspector. The address and phone number can be found in the back of your local yellow pages.

Zoning Violations

A number of home businesses operate outside the law. Home businesses are created every day without checking into the zoning codes in that community. Then again, there are some home businesses that blatantly disregard the law and operate even though they pose a health or safety risk to themselves, others, or animals. Most get away with it because either no one knows about it or the business isn't disturbing anyone.

Zoning complaints usually begin with a phone call from an unhappy neighbor. Perhaps he or she is put out because your customers take all the parking on the street during your Pilates class. Maybe your neighbor is tired of looking at all that equipment you have stored on your driveway for your roofing business. Then again, maybe you run a perfectly private and discrete home business, but your neighbor is still holding a grudge from last summer's block party. If not your neighbor then the complaint could come from a disgruntled customer, a postal carrier, or anyone at all.

A representative from the town or municipality where you live will come to investigate the complaint. If you have not broken any zoning codes then you may resume your business. If, however, you are cited with zoning violations, the zoning department will send you a notice ordering you to stop your business. If you don't heed the warning you can be fined for each day that you are in violation. You could be fined as much as $100 a day.

Things can really start to heat up if you choose to ignore the zoning notice ordering you to stop your business. As a rule, if you ignore the notice and continue running your business, the zoning department will seek an injunction against you. An injunction is an order from a civil court barring you from continuing the violation. Following that you will receive a notice for a hearing. It's not recommended that you ignore an injunction and fail to appear for the hearing because that puts you in contempt of court. Contempt of court means a possible fine and jail time. Do you see where all of this is heading?

Zoning Variances

There are situations where the zoning laws are either outdated or, in your opinion, unfair. In those cases, you can try to seek a variance. A variance is a license that legally makes it permissible for you to do something that is against the law. Obtaining a license can be easy or tricky, depending on where you live. Sometimes a variance amounts to nothing more than completing paperwork while in other places, you might have to plead your case publicly to your city council. Your local government's zoning or planning department can provide additional information.

If you don't want to get started with fighting zoning codes in your town, there are other possibilities to consider. While these possibilities don't apply to all businesses, they may help to spark other types of solutions for your business. For example, in some areas parking is very restricted. In fact, in some towns parking on the street is prohibited at any hour. You operate a party planning business but you can't have clients over for meetings because there is no place to park. In the spirit of making a good impression and appearing professional, meeting at the local diner might not be a great idea. In these situations, you might consider renting a professional office or suite by the hour or reserving meeting rooms in your public library.

There are a number of websites that offer free legal forms for you to copy and download. A good one that we recommend is: Internet Legal Resource Guide at www.ilrg.com.

Business Licenses and Permits

You finally come up with a great idea for a home business, can't wait to get started, and then Whack! You find out that there are a million permits and licenses to get before you get started. Don't get discouraged because not all permits and licenses apply to everybody. For instance, the person who wants to open a home catering business will need different permits than the person who wants to teach yoga in his or her den.

Top 10 List of Most Common
Licenses and Permits

1. Business license
2. Home occupation license
3. Air and water pollution control permit
4. Fire department permit
5. Sign permit
6. Health department permit
7. Seller's permit/sales tax license
8. County licenses
9. State licenses
10. Federal licenses

Business Licenses

Every business, no matter what the size or location, must have a business license issued by the county where that business will be located. Most license fees range from $50 to $125 and are valid for up to three years. If you fail to get a license in a timely manner, you can be fined for late application fees. While your business license is being processed someone from the zoning department will typically come out and do an inspection of your business site.

Home Occupation License

If your local government restricts home-based businesses in your area, you will need to obtain a home occupation license.

Air and Water Pollution Control Permit

Many local, county, and city governments have codes in place to protect its population from air and water pollution. If your business creates gases, discharges waste into the sewers, or burns any kind of materials into the air, it is likely that you will need a permit.

Fire Department Permit

Generally, you will need a fire department permit if you plan to use any flammable products or if your home will be open to the public. What home-based businesses are more likely to require a fire department permit?

- Day care centers
- Home-based dance, exercise, or yoga centers
- Home catering businesses
- Jewelry makers
- Photographers

Sign Permit

There are restrictions on the use of signs for business use. In some communities, signs of any kind, even "for sale" signs, are not permitted. In other communities, there are restrictions on the sign's size, location, lighting, and type.

Health Department

If you intend to handle or sell food in your business, you will need a health department permit. The health department in your area will come out and inspect your equipment and facilities before issuing a permit. In some areas, you might even be required to take a course in the proper handling of food.

County, State, and Federal Licenses and Permits

Any business may have to answer not only to local government but also to county, state, and federal governments as well.

County Permits

If your business falls outside a town or city's jurisdiction, you will need a county permit to do business.

State Licensure

There are many professions and occupations that require licenses or occupational permits. Obtaining a license usually means that the person has passed an examination or completed required course requirements. Typically, the following professions require state licensure:

- Aestheticians
- Auto mechanics
- Barbers
- Building contractors
- Collection agents
- Cosmetologists
- Electricians
- Hair stylists
- Insurance agents
- Mental health professionals (i.e., psychologists, social workers, family therapists)
- Physicians
- Plumbers
- Private investigators
- Real estate brokers
- Repossessors

Federal Licenses

Most home-based businesses do not require a federal license. Those that do require a federal license usually fall under businesses that include meat processing, investment advisories, or radio and TV stations. To find out if your business will require one, contact the Federal Trade Commission (see Appendix A).

Seller's Permit/Sales Tax License

You must pay sales tax if you are a home-based business that sells taxable goods or services to the public. Sales tax is required if you are doing business on a retail level. While many states don't require that service businesses collect sales tax, many are beginning to require it. Both sales tax and sales regulations vary from state to state so be sure to find out what is required in your local area.

It's in your best interest to have your seller's permit before opening up for business. In some states, it is considered a criminal act to operate a business without one. If the state finds out that you haven't been charging sales tax to your customers they can make you pay back everything that should have been charged to your customers.

Most states have a website where you can not only get all the information you need to comply with state laws and regulations, but you can also apply for licenses and permits. For example, Florida has a very good one at www.myflorida.com.

You can find out what is needed in your state by contacting your state's tax department.

Intellectual Properties

You may have heard this term before but weren't sure exactly what it was. When people speak of intellectual properties, they are referring to your ideas and creativity. Intellectual properties may include:

- Art design
- Business logo
- Business name
- Computer programs
- Formulas
- Ingredients in a recipe
- Inventions
- Newspaper and magazine articles
- Photography
- Product designs
- Writing
- Words in a song

Intellectual properties, just like a car or a gold watch, have value, are protected under the law, and can be bought and sold. Why are some intellectual properties more valuable than others? Much depends on the uniqueness of the property and its competitive value in the marketplace.

Intellectual properties are protected from being stolen in four ways: trademarks, patents, trade secrets, and copyrights.

Trademarks

If you are wondering what a trademark is, think about one of your favorite foods or drinks. For example, if you love to eat Wise® Potato Chips then you know that every bag has a yellow and blue owl eye on the front. That logo or trademark for Wise Potato Chips is easily identifiable and distinguishes the product from others

A trademark (^{TM}) can be a:

- Device
- Distinctive word or phrase
- Name
- Symbol

Anybody has the right to put the distinctive symbol (^{TM}) to his or her word, phrase, or logo. But just because you put the trademark symbol there doesn't automatically mean that your work is protected from theft. To legally protect your work, you must register it. Trademarks can be registered in the state where you live if you only seek state protection. However, if you want to protect your trademark across the country, you will need to register it with the U.S. Patent and Trademark Office (USPTO). Fortunately, you can do all this over the Internet at www.uspto.gov. Once your trademark is registered nationally, you stop using the ^{TM} and begin using the ® symbol. If you check back with the owl on the Wise Potato Chips bag, you'll notice the ® at its side.

Along with trademarks, there is also something referred to as service marks (^{SM}). A service mark is a trademark for service indicating that your business name is nationally registered and protected under federal law. Stanley Steamer^{SM}, the carpet cleaner company, is an example of a business using a service mark. The service mark is particularly valuable if you are considering a franchise operation and expanding the business across the country.

This is an important point: Registering your business name within your state is not the same as obtaining a trademark. All businesses must register their names within the state where they plan to do business. If you want your name to have national protection from others using it (or stealing it), then you will need to apply for trademark protection.

How can you find out if someone has already laid claim to a trademark or service mark? The USPTO has a database that you can check at *www.uspto.gov/tmbd/index.*

Why should you register a trademark (^{TM}) or service mark (^{SM})? You should register a trademark or a service mark for federal protection in the event that someone tries to use or steal your work. If you learn that someone has stolen a trademark or service mark, you can obtain federal court orders to make sure he or she stops using your work.

What is the cost of registering a trademark or service mark? To obtain a federally registered trademark or service mark, the fee is $245.

Patents

Patents protect the inventions and works of an inventor from being stolen or copied by somebody else. Patents are not that easy to obtain, and inventions must meet certain qualifications (i.e., it must be new, useful, and not something obvious and ordinary). There are three main types of patents—main, utility, and the most common, the design patent.

A patent on an invention is considered valid for up to 20 years, with the exception of a design patent, which is valid for 14 years. Patents are not renewable, which means that when the 14 years or 20 years are up, you can't prevent anyone from using your invention. A patent in the United States will not protect your invention in other countries. To do that, you will have to file a patent application in every country in which you want protection.

The cost of filing for a patent at the USPTO is approximately $380.

A patent protects not only the invention but prevents others from copying, reproducing, and selling that invention without the consent of the patent owner. A sticky point—just because you hold a patent on an invention doesn't mean that you have permission to sell it. It means that you can prevent others from selling your invention.

What You Can Patent

- *Machines*
- *Major variations in existing products*
- *New varieties of plants*
- *Original designs for manufacturing*
- *Products*
- *Processes*

What You Cannot Patent

- *Business ideas*
- *Mathematical formulas*
- *Printed material*
- *Scientific theories*

If you elect to hire an attorney to help you with patent filing, it's best to find a patent attorney. Patent attorneys are well-versed in intellectual properties and the federal laws protecting patents.

Trade Secrets

Trade secrets are business information that gives you an upper-hand or edge over your competitors. A trade secret may be:

- Customer list
- Formula for cosmetics
- Invention
- Recipes

Copyrights

A copyright does not protect your idea; it protects your expression of an idea. In other words, a copyright prevents people from using an original work of expression such as art, music, and books without the written consent of the copyright owner. It does not, however, protect your idea from being used or stolen.

According to copyright law, an original work is considered automatically copywritten once you put that work into a *fixed* form. Fixed form means that others can see or hear your work. For example, there is a song in your head that you have been humming for months. Finally, you write the song down onto paper, or record it onto disk or tape. A work is considered in a fixed form if it appears on paper, sheet music, disk, manuscript, audiotape, videotape, film, CD, LP, or cassette. Once your work is in one of these formats, it is copyright protected for your lifetime plus 50 years after your death.

A Copyright Protects

- *Architectural works*
- *Artistic works*
- *Choreographic works*
- *Cinema*
- *Dramatic works*
- *Literary works*
- *Musical works*
- *Photography*
- *Software programs*
- *Sound recordings*
- *Video*

A Copyright Does Not Protect

- *Ideas*
- *Names*
- *Short phrases*
- *Titles*
- *Works not in a fixed form*

It is good practice to register your copyrighted work even though it is not required. Use of the copyright notice on your work informs the public that your novel, song, or video is protected by copyright. In other words, your copyright becomes a matter of public record. More importantly, a registered copyright will offer some protection in the event that your work is infringed upon or used without your written consent. If your work carries the proper notice, the person accused of infringement cannot claim that he or she didn't know the work was protected by a copyright:

© 1997 Aimee Walsh

When you place a copyright on your work, you will need to include the following three elements:

1. The symbol for copyright ©, the word *Copyright,* or the abbreviation *Copra*
2. The year of the first publication
3. The name of owner of the copyright

Sound recordings have a slightly different copyright notice—the letter P in a circle. For example:

℗   1998 Isabella Diaz

The registering of a copyright is rather straightforward. In the same envelope, you would send a check for $20 made out to the Copyright Office, a completed application form, and a nonreturnable copy of the work being registered (see Appendix A for more information).

Using Copyrighted Material

When it comes to using someone else's work, there are two things to keep in mind—how much you use and how you use it. Under copyright law there is a concept called *fair use* that permits you to use a small portion of someone else's work without seeking permission. For example, you've been hired to write an article for *DogFancy* magazine on popular breeds of dogs. In your research for the article, you find a list written by another author called, "The Top 10 Breeds in America." Copyright law does not prohibit someone from using data or basic facts. But copyright law does protect that author if you use that list as it exists in his or her article and claim it as your own. In this situation, you have three choices to make: first, you could quote the list directly and credit the author in your article;

second, you could get the author's consent to use the list; and third, you might be better off re-working the basic data in a version that is uniquely your own.

Public Domain

There are some works that belong in the public domain, which means that it is not protected by copyright laws. Anyone can use these works without obtaining permission from the author or creator and his or her heirs. All federal government publications fall under public domain and can be copied freely by anyone. If the copyright of a work has expired than that, too, is considered public domain.

Nondisclosure Agreements

A nondisclosure agreement (NDA) is a document that can protect your designs, business formulas, client lists, trade secrets, and other business-related items from being used or shared by anyone else without your written consent. NDAs are also known as confidentiality agreements.

For instance, you've developed a great line of children's note cards that you would like to show to graphic and printing professionals but you're worried that your clever idea could get stolen. Or perhaps, you've created a natural line of skin care products and you're worried that a manufacturer might use them for their own sales.

Before you show anyone something that you would not want copied or used without your permission, ask the person to sign an NDA. Your NDA should state clearly:

- What you want protected
- That you are showing this product, item, or design in confidence
- The purpose for showing or sharing the product, item, or design with this person or company

It is acceptable for you to create your own NDA, but it's also not a bad idea to run it past your attorney first. An NDA sends a strong statement that you are serious about your work and are prepared to protect it.

e-Commerce

We would be remiss if we didn't address e-commerce or the business of selling on the Internet. If you are interested in selling products from your website, there a few steps to take. First: you will need to find out about the sales tax requirements in your state. To do that, contact your state tax agency. Have you thought about what form of payment you will accept? If you're selling products over the Internet, you had better be set up to accept credit cards. To do that you will need to set up a merchant account. One way to set up a merchant account is by contacting E-Commerce Exchange at *www.ecxweb.com*. If the products you plan to sell are not your own, you may want to consider obtaining a resellers certificate. A resellers certificate gives you access to wholesalers (which means better prices). Finally, people who shop on the Internet like to know that their credit card information is protected and can't be stolen by others. Your customers would want to know that yours is a secure site. You can secure your website by contacting Veri-sign's Secure Server ID program at *http://digitalid.verisign.com/server/index*.

Commonly Asked Legal Questions

1. **How is a copyright different from a trademark and a patent?**
   A copyright protects original works of expression, such as a musical score or a novel, but it does not specifically protect titles, names, or short phrases. A trademark protects logos, symbols, slogans, and distinctive words or phrases that distinguish a product in the marketplace. A patent stops the commercial use of inventions and new ideas from being used without the written consent of the patent owner.

2. **I have a great idea for a screenplay. Can I copyright it so no one will steal it?**
   A screenplay or any other work (literature, music, art, etc.) can only be copyrighted when it is placed in a fixed form. In the case of your screenplay, fixed form means that the screenplay exists on paper. Once your screenplay is in a fixed form, a copyright is automatically assumed; however, that does not mean that someone can't take your ideas behind the screenplay. The actual copyright only protects

your screenplay as it exists in fixed form and not the ideas associated with it.

3. **How can you protect a trade secret?**
   First of all, if you have something special that you don't want stolen, then by all means, be very careful who sees it. If you have been very careful about sharing a recipe, ingredient, or an invention and another person discloses that information to others, you do have the right to sue that person. Additionally, you may be able to stop them from using your trade secret and collect for damages. It is important that you ask anyone who is about to see your trade secret to sign an NDA, which declares that he or she will not disclose or use your trade secret. If the individual breaks the signed agreement, you have the right to pursue legal action. Be cautious when dealing with large corporations—they're bigger than you and often have more leverage. You can assume that they have a first-rate legal department. Our advice when negotiating with major companies is to have an expert intellectual property attorney by your side. (Remember Kathy's near disaster with the well-known publisher?)

4. **I've created a software program that I would like to sell to the public. Should I look into licensing my program?**
   Yes, you should license your software program if you plan to profit from its creation. A license will spell out how you want your software used and under what conditions. A license will also state how you will be compensated for your software program. Like the NDA, it is wise to have your attorney draft this licensing agreement for you.

5. **Do you have to collect sales tax when you sell items out-of-state?**
   If you are selling an item (i.e., book, gift basket, brow shaver) in a mail order catalog then you are not required to charge a sales tax outside your own state. For example, if you live in New Jersey and sell gift baskets through the mail to people in Iowa, you do not need to collect sales tax. The same rule applies to the Internet where you only have to collect sales tax on individuals living in your state. The exception to this rule is if you have sales representation to customers in other states. If, for instance, you have a gift rep in Maryland,

Georgia, and Virginia, then you would need to collect sales tax in those states.

Keeping Your Eye on the Prize

Try not to let the details of starting a home business discourage you from going for your dream. While there are many important details to address, they can be tackled—one at a time. Use the checklist provided in Chapter 7 as a guide. Keep all your paperwork in one place so that everything stays together. Keep in mind that not all the permits and licenses mentioned in this chapter will apply to you. The good news is that with every point you check off the list, you are one step closer to working from home.

CHAPTER 10

INSURANCE IN THE HOME OFFICE

Insurance needs of home office workers vary. If you are starting your own business, you may want health insurance and life insurance—those benefits you used to received when you worked for an outside firm. However, even telecommuters will want to be sure they have certain kinds of insurance to cover equipment and other items they may have in their home. It's impossible for any book to cover all aspects of insurance for every possible need. That's why we recommend you meet with a financial planner or insurance broker and at least listen and gauge what they may have to say about your specific needs. However, here are some basics to get you started.

Health Insurance

Much as we all like to complain about the era of "managed care," most of us want and need health insurance of some sort. The problem is that as a nation, we are woefully underinsured and uninsured. People who start home businesses are a perfect example. If covering a family, for instance, the costs can go quite high, and it may seem like something you can put off until your business is fully self-supporting. Erica's yearly health insurance for her family, not even dental and life, tops out right now at over $13,000. Off the top. Yes, that's a real figure.

No wonder people skimp on insurance or cut corners at times. However, we don't need to regale you with horror stories of uninsured people to have you know that you need insurance of some sort one way or the other.

When you leave a place of employment, you will be offered COBRA. This allows you to pay for insurance through your old company for a period of 18 months. What is usually a rude awakening is the price. Buried in your paycheck with all those little numbers like FICA and taxes was probably a number for health insurance representing your portion, with the company picking up the tab for the rest. That new number can carry quite a bit of "sticker" shock.

One of the advantages of incorporating is it allows you to be treated like a corporation and get bids for insurance. The menus of options are extensive: HMOs, PPOs, more traditional 80/20 plans, and so forth. Again, only you and your family and an adviser can know your needs.

Another option, if you don't incorporate, is to get insurance through a membership you might have, such as writers' guilds. The problem with this option is the guild can be dropped from coverage or switch, and you don't have much of a say in it.

One option worth discussing here is called "catastrophe" insurance. For a greatly reduced price, you won't be covering your doctor visits, well-baby care, or even the initial fees at a hospital emergency ward. However, should a catastrophe happen, such as a serious operation or heaven forbid cancer or another long-term, serious illness, this type of coverage "kicks in" when the total bills hit a number such as $5,000. While this in and of itself might sound expensive, if you are in good health and rarely go to the doctor's, as you are starting out it *may* be a better choice than no coverage at all.

Another item to keep in mind as you get bids is if you are sure you are through having children, are a woman and truly post-menopause, or have opted for sterilization as a form of birth control, or are an unmarried male, coverage for any type of health insurance without OB/maternity is also much cheaper. Remember to explore this with any agent.

Long-Term Disability

Many large companies and some smaller ones cover long- and short-term disability. This coverage allows you to stay out of work in case of a long illness or an accident, or for maternity leave coverage. It tends to be one of those coverages that you may overlook if you start your own home-based company.

This type of insurance is, again, not likely to be cheap. You may also, literally, not be able to obtain it if you have a pre-existing condition. Erica has a serious health problem and has been told by numerous agents in no uncertain terms that despite her company's healthy yearly bank account, no one will ever give her long-term disability coverage in case she has to be out sick or hospitalized for any length of time. Had she had the foresight to buy this coverage *prior* to her diagnosis, this would not be the case.

Again, it would be wonderful if we could advise you "Insure yourself to the hilt so *any eventuality* is covered." However, particularly if you are truly starting out in a new business, this isn't likely to be advice that is financially easy to heed.

Home and Renters' Insurance

Starting a business with equipment or technology around? Don't allow yourself to be caught without coverage in case of fire, flood, or theft, and this bears reminding for renters, who are much less likely to have this coverage.

However, don't think that if such a fire, flood, or theft occurred that the insurance company is going to hand you a big, fat check. Have you *documented* your equipment, especially technology equipment?

One wise way to document your possessions is to take multiple photographs of every room and all the items in it. Another is to make a video. However, you would perhaps be surprised to learn where people *keep* this documentation. In the very house that is now flooded or has caught on fire. Documenting your possessions and equipment is very important. Then you need to store that documentation, ideally in two spots. Keep one in a bank safety deposit box and the other with a friend or relative where you can get your hands on it quickly. Double documentation is a nice safety valve.

What about technology aspects of your coverage? While it is terrific if you photograph your laptop or computer, better yet to keep the receipt and serial numbers in a safe spot too, so you can prove what you paid for it. You may also, surprisingly, in your homeowners' policy, have some built-in coverage for surges that cause equipment failure. This may be something to ask your agent about.

Life Insurance

No one likes to talk about life insurance. Unpleasant. Nonetheless, when starting a new business, it's very important that you assess your life insurance needs. One reason is, again, that old paycheck you used to have at a company. Hidden there among FICA and so on may have been some "automatic" coverage at a specific multiplication of your salary.

Like health insurance, there are many different configurations of life insurance, and only someone familiar with your full financial needs can advise you. However, people have a tendency to underinsure, particularly if they have families. One reason is that, for instance, a million dollars may sound like a boatload of money to some. The insurer may feel "That's enough for my husband/wife to live on and to put two kids through college." Likely true. However, if said husband or wife needs to return to the office (e.g., a stay-at-home Mom needs to get a job), what about paying for child care or a nanny for the kids? What about all the survivor's myriad financial needs, not just for a few years but into retirement?

There are two general types of life insurance:

1. Whole (which has cash trade-in value and is more expensive)
2. Term (which is less expensive but has no trade-in value)

Rates will depend on your age, health habits (smokers pay more), occupation (a race car driver pays more than a teacher), and hobbies (skydiving is a no-no).

Finding an Agent/Insurance

We generally advise people to find an insurance agent who represents more than one product or company. Agents who have relationships with multiple insurance carriers can offer you more choices. Also ask other small businesses or work-at-home types for recommendations. You want someone honest, and, in turn, you need to be honest with the agent in order for him or her to best assess your needs. If the first agent you call, for instance, "rates" you poorly (i.e., says you cannot qualify for the best rates because of certain risk or health problems), then call around. Agents tend to compete with each other. Erica was rated poorly by one major company, but another top company gave her its best rates.

As you can see, insurance has multiple layers and ins-and-outs. Assess your own needs honestly, and don't neglect this important element in your 60-second commute.

CHAPTER 11

PINK SLIP BLUES

Fired. Laid-off. Downsized. Excessed. Enron'ed. These words can sting plenty when they describe you. No matter how much you hated the commute, disliked the company, or despised the boss, you probably would have liked to leave on your own terms and not with a pink slip in hand.

Did you ever consider that losing your job just might be the best thing that ever happened to you? Didn't your mother ever tell you that when one door closes, another one opens? What if your best opportunity is just through the next door? Would you ever have taken the chance to work from a home office if you weren't kicked out the corporate door?

The Party's Over

Well, it appears that the great 1990s party is winding down. Pink slips are being handed out faster in corporate America than you can say, "Recession? What recession?" It was quite a party while it lasted. Fantastic bonuses. Posh corporate parties in five-star resorts with unlimited expenses and celebrity entertainment. Never before in the history of this country had so many millionaires at such a young age (many under 30) been made so fast. In certain parts of the country, particularly those rich with tech industries, such as the northeast, southwest, and in California, real estate prices soared through the roof. One reason was the demand for housing, but the other was that those who needed the housing were willing and able to pay anything to get it—and in cash.

If you cruise through the major business magazine websites such as *Forbes* and *Fortune*, you might notice a disturbing addition to the sites—a layoff posting for the major corporations. Even the kids out in Silicon Valley don't look so cheerful these days. They were the ones willing to work day and night for the promise of big bonuses and stock options. Many of the dot.coms were so eager to harness this youthful ambition that they encouraged them to bring their pets to work, dress comfortably, and play foozball in the break room.

60 Seconds with Mac Angle

Mac Angle works as a Human Resources Director for ITC Corp., a small start-up IT company. He works almost exclusively through the Internet in his home office as there isn't a big need for outside office space. In fact, most of the employees communicate through the company's website. The company does maintain a small administrative office for face-to-face situations but aside from that everyone works from home. While Mac prefers to work from his home office, the one thing that drives him crazy are interruptions—and they occur whether you work in a traditional office or in your home. As Mac says, "It may be a phone call, or the dog needs to go out. Interruptions always occur, just a different type."

One Silicon Valley website used to gleefully post the Bill Gates wealth-o-meter. That's gone. It seems that the days when the dot.coms pushed the NASDAQ to record highs are gone, perhaps for good. It's estimated that when the dot.coms and IPOs imploded, there was a loss of over $1 trillion in market value. That was followed by the implosion of the telecoms. Thousands of people, young and old, found themselves out of work and without benefits or retirement plans.

Many other hard-working people in the manufacturing and travel industries have been handed their pink slips—people who dutifully worked their whole lives for one company only to see retirements disappear into dust.

Trouble in Paradise

If you haven't lost your job but fear that the pink slip could be just around the corner, here a few signs that trouble may be brewing in your company:

- **Executive management is leaving the company**—If the senior executives are leaving, chances are good that the ship's going down.
- **Your company has issued a hiring or overtime freeze**—Raises are pushed back and job openings are not being filled.
- **Travel cutbacks**—People are being told to stay close to the office and teleconference instead of traveling to meetings and conferences.
- **Expense reductions**—No more luncheons or dinners with clients.
- **Support staff is thinning out**—This means you are going to have to make do with less.

Another clue is how the competition is doing. If the competition is already reducing staff, restructuring, or losing many of its top management, then the chances are pretty good that your company will follow suit.

Companies tighten their financial belts all the time. Consider AT&T—they lay off people by the thousands and yet continue to churn onward. American Airlines periodically makes a clean sweep of its upper management, but they're still dominating the skies. However, if you see several signs at once, such as hiring freezes, management layoffs, and budget cuts, you just might want to dust off your resume. If you feel the inevitable is coming, start preparing before you're escorted from the building.

What to Do BEFORE You Lose Your Job

If you can sense that your job is in trouble, there are few important measures to take before you're handed the pink slip, such as:

1. Take advantage of everything your company has to offer while you still have it. That includes:
   - Health examinations for you and the family (medical, dental, and vision)
   - Professional training (workshops, conferences)
2. Get your financial house in order.
   - Bring down your credit card balances
   - Eliminate excess spending where you can
   - Investigate where you can get funds (money, loans) if you need them
   - Make sure your pension and 401-Ks are protected (and it's all not in company stock)
   - Make sure that your life insurance benefits are protected
   - Review your benefits package and make sure the information is correct
   - Put aside some cash from your check each week
   - Consider a part-time moonlighting position
3. Construct a plan of what you will do when the inevitable happens
   - Contact head hunters
   - Rework your resume

- Broaden your skills with some college or professional courses
- Go through your Rolodex and make sure you have your contacts in order
- Network with others in the industry and learn where new opportunities exist

4. Consider starting your own business from home

- Research the market
- Visit lenders (banks, venture capitalists)
- Write a business plan
- Visit a SCORE office for free advice from retired executives or contact a SBA office (for more information, see Appendix A).

Your First Five Steps After Losing Your Job

If you've never lost a job, the experience can be very unsettling, particularly in corporate America because their sendoffs can be quite chilly. For instance, it is not unusual to come to work one day and find that your keys no longer open your office. Maybe you arrive to find a rather menacing looking security guard standing in front of your office. He'll ask for your I.D. badge and keys and then tell you that you've got 15 minutes to pack up. To make matters more strange and embarrassing, the guard will walk you to your car. How's that for a kick in the teeth?

If you've got that pink slip in your hand, then it is time to get busy. Of course it smarts and you feel bad. Shake it off. You've got better things to do than feel sorry for yourself.

Step 1: The First Issue is Money

One minute you had a steady paycheck and the next, you don't. Contact your state unemployment office as soon as possible to arrange for unemployment benefits. Clearly, these checks won't match those you received at your job, but it is money, and it is yours. Until you get settled into another job, consider yourself in survival mode. If you're like the rest of us, you have rent or mortgage payments, car loans, and you probably require food to live.

Step 2: You'll Need Health Insurance

Don't walk around for one minute without health insurance if it is at all unavoidable. Often the group insurance at work can be converted to an individual package at rates that are manageable. If you work in the United States, you may be covered by COBRA (the Consolidated Omnibus Budget Reconciliation Act of 1985). COBRA requires that your employer allow you to stay with the company's health insurance for a period of 18 months or more for the same rates that the other employees are paying.

Step 3: Contact a Temp Agency

Open your yellow page directory and look under employment. You will be amazed at the number of temp agencies listed. Temp agencies have become big business in the past few years because many companies realize that it is cheaper to hire temporary employees than to hire permanent employees and pay their benefits. Chances are excellent that a temp agency will be able to find work for you. The good news is that sometimes these placements lead to permanent positions or a new career path. For a listing of national temp agencies, see Appendix B.

Step 4: Write the Company
a Thank You Letter

Did we hear you mutter something under your breath? You heard us correctly—write your company's CEO a thank you letter. You may have been fired, but you don't want to blow up any bridges as you're leaving. Thank the company for the opportunity to work there, be part of their team, and for all the valuable experience you acquired while you were there. Don't forget to keep a copy of this letter or to request that it be placed in your file. If you know the CEO personally or work directly under him or her be sure to have a brief meeting before you leave.

Step 5: Stay in the Loop

Now is not the time to take a cross-country road tour. If you had a good relationship with your immediate boss or even your boss's boss then keep in touch with them. He or she is often the next to go and will sometimes get another job before you—which is when he or she can be helpful. Rework your resume, and make a list of friends and contacts in your industry. The Internet is loaded with leads to track in your job hunt. You can consult on-line with head hunters, post your resume on career websites, and arrange to have e-mail sent to you whenever a job pops up that matches your job description. Don't roll up the sidewalk and become a recluse. Remember—network, network, network.

Don't Be Bamboozled

You may have lost your job but you haven't lost your mind. No matter how stressed or anxious you feel, you need to keep your wits about you. Plenty of people have been coaxed down the path that looks too good to be true and lost their life savings. Work-

According to the National Fraud Information Center, work-at-home business scams are the #1 source of fraud in the country.

ing four jobs is better than becoming involved in any of the following schemes.

Free Information

Ask yourself, why would someone work so hard just to give you something for free? Is that how they stay in business, by giving away free information? The free information they want to send you would make a better liner in your son's hamster cage. The real information that you want is going to cost you. See the hook?

Starter Kits

Think about this for a moment—a starter kit that you buy on television or at a job fair for $29.95 is going to reveal all the secrets of the industry and make you a successful business person? If anything could be learned from a starter kit, then why would anyone go to school? The bottom line is that there is nothing in these starter kits that can't be found for free at the public library, on the Internet, or by doing some homework. Another tempting starter kit is the one that contains the materials for you to make your own Christmas ornaments or cat collars. What you usually receive is a box filled with beads along with some undecipherable instructions.

"900" Numbers

This may be one of the best scams around. For a limited time and for just $1.99 a minute, you can speak to one of their experts about how to buy homes in foreclosure or sell ice to Eskimos. The minute you dial the 900 number, you are getting billed. Often the lines are busy and you're put on hold for 10 or 20 minutes or more. All the while the charges are adding up at the 900 number rate. The expert? He or she is probably sitting in a condo somewhere in Hoboken, New Jersey, along with 10 other people, and reading off information from a script.

The Flyers Tucked on Your Windshield

You come out of the supermarket and there's this colorful flyer jammed under your windshield wiper. It says, "Earn big money working from home, no experience necessary." The reality is most likely that someone is trying to lure you into working for a 900 number, joining a pyramid scheme, or becoming a one-person sweat shop.

Pyramid Schemes

These are typically scams set up to look like real businesses that require you to recruit other people to join the pyramid—for a fee. Pyramid schemes are illegal in most states because there is no product or service being sold. The only people who are making any money are the ones who created the pyramid. Eventually the scheme collapses and everyone on the lower tiers of the pyramid is out his or her investment.

Multilevel Marketing

Multilevel marketing (MLM), also known as network marketing, can resemble a pyramid because to make money you have to sell products and recruit others under you to do the same. A MLM often asks for an initial investment that includes products and sales materials. There are several highly successful and well-known multilevel companies such as Amway, Avon, Mary Kay Cosmetics, and Tupperware that are legitimate.

A red flag should go up if the multilevel company is more interested in recruiting than in selling products. In that case, the MLM could actually be a pyramid scheme.

Glowing Testimonials

Have you ever watched late night television? Then you may have seen those infomercials in which person after person gleefully swears that they've become financially independent by joining this company or taking these seminars. Usually the person is in south Florida cruising down the Intracoastal Waterway on a yacht. Do yourself a favor—either change the channel or go to sleep.

If these opportunities sound too good to be true, they are. Unfortunately, many people get scammed every day because they were bamboozled by phony ads and get-rich-quick schemes. Before you invest in something that sounds fast and easy, do your homework and check it out thoroughly.

Red Flags for a Possible Scam

Often the first sense you get that something is a scam is in your gut, but you decide to ignore it because the people seem friendly and sincere—and you'd like to make some extra income. If you suspect that the business opportunity isn't legitimate, do some snooping with the following authorities:

- Better Business Bureau—There should be a local office in your community. They will be able to tell you if anyone has reported a complaint or if there are pending lawsuits against them. You can find your local bureau listed in your telephone directory.

- Post Office—The U.S. Postal Service tracks mail fraud. Visit your local post office and discuss your concerns with the postmaster. He or she can probably provide helpful information for recognizing fraudulent mail activities.

 Write this down...

The National Fraud Information Center provides up-to-date information on frauds and scams. To get information or to report a suspected scam, contact: The National Fraud Information Center, P.O. Box 65868, Washington, DC 20035, (800) 876-7060, www.fraud.org

Turning Lemons into Lemonade

As we mentioned at the beginning, getting your pink slip might be the best thing that ever happened to you. It may be your opportunity to finally do what you really love or even to work from a home office. If you find yourself at this crossroads, it is a terrific time to take inventory of your skills and talents.

Schedule a meeting with yourself and clear out a few quiet hours in a place where you can think and take some notes. During the weekdays the public library or even the cafés at Barnes & Noble or Borders are wonderful places to sit uninterrupted and brainstorm. Allow yourself the time to think freely and creatively about the kind of work or careers that you're most interested in. The added bonus of a library or a bookstore is that you can prowl through books, directories, and magazines to get more information. Try to come away with at least five jobs or businesses to pursue.

Once you've got a list of potential jobs, it's time to do some serious homework and market research. For example, if you are interested in purchasing a franchise business then investigate:

- The market for trends and longevity of this business
- Initial investment and start-up costs
- Potential locations and customers
- Skills necessary to run the franchise

- Others who successfully own one of these franchises
- Potential money lenders
- Earning potential

Perhaps you've decided that all you really want to do is work for yourself as a consultant in your industry. For instance, if you are a biomedical engineer and you want to consult from a home office then you might investigate:

- The current market trends in the industry
- The companies that are interested in outside consultants
- Others who successfully consult from a home office
- Typical consulting fees and services

Finally, lay out a step-by-step plan that includes a timetable and goals. You may decide that while you are developing a business it is necessary to moonlight in order to pay the bills. You may decide to rejoin the job market and develop your plan slowly. Remember that it takes a while; in some cases it can take over two years for new businesses to get off the ground.

Getting a pink slip is never pleasant. In this economy it seems that more and more pink slips are being handed out every day. You'll have good days when you're raring to go and days when you want to pull the blanket over your head. All of those reactions are normal. Take those first steps to ensure that you have an income and health insurance. Lean on your friends and family when you need to and by all means stay in touch with those who can be helpful. And remember to network, network, network. (For some great networking ideas, visit Chapter 15, Marketing Your Business.)

CHAPTER 12

CHILD CARE:
LIFE ON THE HIGH WIRE

Child care is a consideration whether you work outside the home or in a home office. The kind of child care you choose depends a great deal on the kind of work you do and how much your budget will allow. The right child care can be a real boost to your family and your life. You know that the kids are well-supervised and you can get some work done. In this chapter, we're going to discuss child care options and how to make the best decision for you and your children.

Can You Go it Alone?
Deciding whether or not you need outside help with your children is a personal decision and one that only you can make. You know what feels comfortable, what you can juggle, and what you can afford. Although we have five children between us, we decided that we could get along without a full-time nanny or babysitter in our homes. Far from being superwomen, we could do without the help because of the kind of work we each do. Unlike a sales or marketing position that requires you to be available on the telephone, we write and edit books. While there are constant deadlines to be met, we have some flexibility in how and when we work. When the children were very young, we would do the most demanding work during naps and in the evening. When the children entered nursery school, we had mornings, nap time and evenings to work. Sound blissful? Sometimes the plan worked well, and at other times it blew up in our faces.

The My Time, Your Time, Our Time Rule
From an early age, we taught our children an important rule. The children were taught that there is "my time" or the time when mom works and needs some quiet and some space, "your time" when mom does the things the children want, and "our time" when the kids and mom do things together. To keep an eye on our kids, we often set up space in our home offices so that they could play quietly (that's a lie) around us. In Kathy's office, she set up a small child's picnic table so that her son could color, do puzzles, and build while she worked at her desk.

60 Seconds with AnneMarie Walsh

Artist and author of *A Mother's Wisdom*, AnneMarie had her challenges in raising two boys, Tommy and Matthew, as she was trying to complete her book. One day while working from her home office, AnneMarie was ambushed by her sons and 10 of their closest buddies. Pushed out of the office, she went and sat down in a child's rocking chair and tried to continue where she had left off. Suddenly there was screaming at the front door. It seems her son Matthew's friend was afraid of dogs and took off down the street at the sight of their bassett hound puppy. The pup, in turn, took off after the young boy. When AnneMarie tried to get up from the tiny rocking chair, she found herself quite stuck. Concerned that the little boy could trip or get hurt, AnneMarie raced out the front door with the rocking chair tightly wrapped around her tail end. This is a story her boys still love to tell to anyone who might listen.

For Erica, her office is directly off the living room. She set the kids up with toys, a video, and some snacks on those days when a project had to be finished.

Both of us learned quickly that when children are underfoot or under your desk, be prepared for the unexpected. Sometimes no matter how well you try to coordinate work and children, it all will backfire. (For sanity-saving suggestions on what to do when all else fails, see Plan B in Chapter 4.) Like the day Erica's kids covered the dog in Post-its or the day

If you are concerned about your children going out a door without you hearing them, try hanging bells on your door knobs and sliding glass doors. The jingle of those bells will alert you that a door is being opened.

Kathy's daughter drew all over her body with a permanent black marker and proudly presented herself to mom during a meeting—naked. But those incidents were fun and fixable and often pretty hilarious. The bottom line for us is that we are both okay with chaos even on those days when it doesn't feel so funny. The reason is that we see it as a tradeoff. We made the decision to deal with the interruptions and the pandemonium rather than to work away from our children. That is a compromise that works well for us most of the time, but it may not work well for others. Some people don't have the temperament for shenanigans—and you probably know who you are. Others have jobs that don't permit constant interruptions and background noises. It all depends on what your job is and what "environmental" conditions you can tolerate.

Here is a fast checklist to help you decide whether or not you can go it alone. Keep in mind that deciding whether or not to have help is not a test for good parenting. Don't feel guilty if you need a quiet, empty house a few hours a day to get your work done.

	Yes	No
1. Am I required to work a traditional 9 to 5 day?	___	___
2. Are my children home all day?	___	___
3. Do I have a child under three years old?	___	___
4. Does my business depend on being available to take phone calls (i.e., realtor, publicist)?	___	___
5. Do I live near water (i.e., pool, canal, lake) or high up with a terrace or balcony?	___	___
6. Would it hurt my professional image if children's voices were heard in the background?	___	___
7. Would I describe my child as particularly active?	___	___
8. Am I able to work at night or when the kids have gone to bed?	___	___
9. Does my job involve deadlines?	___	___
10. Does my job involve the handling of anything that could be dangerous to a child (i.e., heat, chemicals)?	___	___

Sometimes it is easier to make a decision when you see it in black and white. Take a look at your yes and no responses and see if your answers shed some light on what you need. If you live near water (that includes your pool) and have a job that demands you be on the phone and you have an active toddler, then it is wise to either (a) get some help in the house or (b) enroll your child in a program for a few hours a day. On the other hand, if your job involves writing or graphics, the hours are flexible, and your child is enrolled in preschool, then you can probably make do without help or babysitters. As we all know too well, children can get into mischief in about 10 seconds. What really matters when making the decision to go it alone or to get some help is the safety and well-being of your children.

How Do You Know What You Need?

Before you can decide on the kind of child care you will choose, figure out what you require and how much you can afford. Child care is an expensive

proposition but one that may help you to get ahead at work or firmly establish your home business. Take a look at this child care worksheet and use it
to see what option makes the most sense for you.

- How many children do you have? _____
- How old are your children? _____
- How many days do you need coverage? _____
- How many hours in a day do you need coverage? _____
- Do your children have special needs? _____
    Allergies _____
    Transportation to afternoon specials _____
    Homework supervision _____
    Special dietary needs _____
    Physical, emotional, medical, or mental concerns _____
- Do you travel often? _____
- Do you have evening meetings? _____
- Do you need someone to provide transportation
  for the kids?_____
- Do you need someone to prepare meals for the kids?_____
- Do you want child care in your home? _____
- Do you want child care outside your home? _____
- Does your work permit interruptions? _____
- Does your work require you to spend a lot of time
  on the phone? _____
- How much can you afford to pay each week? _____

Ultimately, the kind of child care you choose for your children will depend
on how much you can afford and your comfort level. As parents, we are not
the same. Some of us are at ease about nannies or au pairs in our homes,
while others see it as an expensive invasion of privacy. Some prefer the structure and consistency of a day care center while others feel it's too formal a
setting for young children. Still others will only allow a trusted family member to care for their young children. It all depends on what makes sense to
you in your world.

As your children grow, your child care needs will change. Both Erica and Kathy's children are now in school all day so tripping over pull-toys and sippie cups is a thing of the past. Late afternoons can be a bear, but those are the hours that neither one of us expect to get much accomplished. Instead, we're picking kids up from school, shuffling them off to afternoon specials, running errands, supervising homework, and making dinner. (That's all.)

The Menu of Child Care Options

If you are considering child care for your children, there are several options to choose from:

- Afterschool programs
- Au pair
- Babysitter
- Babysitting co-op
- Day care center
- Family and friends
- Family day care
- Mother's day out programs
- Mother's helper
- Nanny (live-in or live-out)
- Play dates
- Siblings
- Tot drops

As you can see from the list, there are many options to think about when it comes to child care. Costs vary across the country depending on where you live and whether you live in the city, the suburbs, or in a rural area. Anticipate that child care costs will be higher when you have an infant, a toddler, or more than one child. You may be familiar with some of the choices on the list, such as fam-

How Can You Find a Good Babysitter or Mother's Helper?

- *Ask your friends who they use or if they know someone.*
- *Your public library may keep a list of teens who have taken babysitting courses.*
- *Contact the job office at local colleges and universities.*
- *Contact sorority houses at local colleges and universities.*
- *Contact places of worship in your community.*
- *Place an ad in your local newspaper or parenting magazine.*
- *Ask your children's teachers if they babysit.*

ily babysitters or siblings watching younger siblings, but others may not be as obvious, such as tot drops, babysitting co-ops, or au pairs.

The Difference Between a Nanny and an Au Pair

Nannies, au pairs, who can keep it all straight? While both provide child care, there are some important differences between the two. The phrase au pair is French and means an arrangement in which services are exchanged on an even basis. For example, an au pair helps out with the children in exchange for room and board and the opportunity to live in a foreign country. Although there are American au pairs, most au pairs are young European women between the ages of 18 and 26. Finding an au pair and making the arrangements for her to work in your home is usually done with the help of an au pair agency. Unlike most nannies, an au pair is not an employee in your household. Au pair agreements state that he or she work a 45-hour week, reside in your home, and return to his or her native country in one year. The cost of an au pair depends on experience and education level. If an au pair has two years experience and has a degree in child development she will be more expensive than one who is less experienced.

The Cost of an Au Pair

An au pair provides child care to your children in exchange for the opportunity to spend a year in another country.
Average cost estimates:

Agency fee range	$4000 to mid $5000
Application fee for agency	$250
Travel expenses for au pair	$300
Weekly "pocket money"*	$139.05 for an au pair with limited experience
	$200 for an au pair with two or more years experience
Education fee	$500

*The weekly "pocket money" salaries are regulated by the U.S. Department of State in accordance with the Fair Labor Standards Act.

For a listing of au pair agencies that meet federal guidelines, see Appendix B at the back of the book.

A nanny is typically a woman, although there are some male nannies, who either lives in your home or travels to your home each day to care for your children. The term "nanny" is tossed about freely and most anyone who looks after children can say that he or she is a nanny. However, there are professionally trained nannies who have studied child development, early education, CPR, nutrition, and first aid and hold diplomas from certified nanny programs. (Contact information for the American Council of Nanny Schools can be found in Appendix B.) A nanny can be found through a professional agency, an ad in the newspaper, or by word of mouth. A nanny's responsibilities in your home could be bathing and dressing your children; getting them ready for school; preparing meals; and shuffling the kids between school, specials, birthday parties, and doctor's appointments. While a nanny may do some light housekeeping, he or she is not considered a housekeeper.

If you search for a nanny via a professional nanny agency, you will be charged a placement fee ranging from $350 to several thousand dollars. Often that fee covers background searches, health examinations, and training. Some nanny agencies are more than simply referral businesses. Some agencies will maintain the nanny as their own employee and will assume responsibility for his or her health insurance and workers compensation, distribute a W-2 form, and file tax information to the IRS.

Be cautious and don't assume that all nanny agencies are created equal. In other words, there are some agencies that are ethical and properly screen each candidate while others say they do when sometimes they don't. An agency is "supposed" to investigate a candidate's health, employment history, references, criminal record, and motor vehicle record. Keep in mind that this is a business that makes money when a nanny is placed. Ask for several references and by all means call them all. You probably should ask the agency about the company that conducted their background checks to verify that your nanny candidate has been properly investigated. A nanny agreement with a professional agency should stipulate that your nanny will be replaced if he or she does not work out in your home. It's never a bad idea to ask around to see if anyone has ever had a bad experience with the agency.

The Cost of a Nanny

Nannies come in two types—live-in or live-out. In general, a nanny's salary can range from $250 to over $700 per week depending on:

- Years of experience as a nanny
- The number of children under his or her charge

- Whether your nanny will live-in or live-out
- Whether or not your nanny requires health insurance

Taxable Nanny

As discussed earlier, there are important differences between nannies and au pairs. While the au pair is not considered an employee in your home, the nanny clearly can be depending on the arrangement. If he or she is not an employee of an agency then you are the employer. Where there is an employee, there are taxes. If you are the nanny's employer, you are responsible for not only paying taxes, but also frequently a good deal more:

- Social Security and Medicare taxes (FICA)
- Federal unemployment taxes (FUTA)
- Filing a W-2 form for your nanny
- Obtaining a federal employer number (EIN) from the IRS
- Reporting wages and taxes relevant to the nanny under Schedule H or "Household Employment Taxes"
- Reporting taxes paid in relation to your nanny on your Form 1040 which is filed together with your Schedule H

The IRS requires that you pay taxes for your nanny if he or she has been paid $1,100 by you in the past year or if he or she was paid $1,000 or more in any calendar quarter in the past two years.

Now you may be saying to yourself, "Wait a minute, I know plenty of people who hire nannies, and they don't go through all this." You are right, they don't. The fact of the matter is that many, many people hire nannies, often as illegal aliens, and pay them "under the table" or strictly in cash so that there is nothing traceable for the IRS. The problem is that it is illegal to hire an illegal alien or a person who has entered the United States illegally—even if you don't know that the person is an illegal alien. The other problem is that it is illegal to not pay taxes.

You may also hear people say that nannies are independent contractors and should be responsible for reporting and paying his or her own taxes. Here's a news flash from the IRS: Nannies are not independent contractors. A nanny is a household employee because you decide his or her salary, pay schedule, hours at work, and the way in which he or she will carry out their duties.

If you hire a person to be a nanny in your home, think of him or her as you would an employee of your company. Except in this case, the company is your family. Like a company, you are expected to pay state and federal taxes. For a clear, step-by-step explanation we suggest you obtain a copy of IRS Publication 926: *Household Employer's Tax Guide.* The fastest way to obtain this publication is to visit the IRS website at *www.irs.gov.*

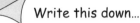

Write this down...

First—What's the big deal about not reporting a nanny's salary to the IRS? It's not a big deal as long as you don't mind the possibility of being prosecuted for tax evasion. As a crime, tax evasion is punishable by fines (what else) and imprisonment.

Second—It is illegal for you to knowingly or unknowingly hire or employ an illegal alien. Contact the Immigration and Naturalization Service at 1-800-870-3676 and ask for their Handbook for Employers.

The Difference Between Family Day Care and Day Care Centers

The primary difference between family day care and a day care center is location. Family day care is where young children are cared for in someone's home. Often the number of children is small, perhaps two or three at a time, or just one family of children at a time. There are more professional family care centers, still housed in a home, but where there might be as many as 12 children and two adults. Although the setting can be cozy and economical, there are a few issues to consider: you could be caught without a place to bring your child if the day care provider is not feeling well, if there's been a death in that person's family, or during holidays. In this situation, you would have to make other plans for those days or that week. Another consideration is that even though the person may be terrific and wonderful with your children, his or her home may not be a licensed family day care center. Licensed family day care centers are expected to operate under the strict guidelines set up by the state, county, or both regarding the health and safety of the children in that center, and the training of those working there.

A day care center is a more formal center where the children are grouped according to age and supervised by trained staff. Day care centers frequently open early in the morning and close some time after the supper hour. Day care centers are usually open during holidays. Though not as relaxed as someone's home, day care centers are required to be licensed and regulated. The staff frequently receives training in CPR, first aid, and age-appropriate activities for children.

The downside to both the family care center and the day care center is that your children may be exposed to other children's colds and infections.

Tot Drops and Mother's Day Out

A tot drop is just as it sounds—a place where you can drop your child off for a few hours at a time. Most tot drops are located in churches, synagogues, community organizations, and sometimes nursery schools. Unlike a day care center, a tot drop operates on a first-come, first-serve basis. A tot drop works well if you occasionally need to drop your child off for two or three hours, but it doesn't work if you need a place on a regular basis. Tot drops are typically staffed by volunteers and college or high school students and supervised by one on-staff person.

Mother's Day Out is also a group placement at a church, synagogue, or community center for a few hours each week. However, Mother's Day Out is different than a tot drop in that you usually need to commit or register your child for a semester or session.

Babysitting Co-Op

The most unusual child care arrangement and perhaps the most difficult to find is the babysitting co-op. A babysitting co-op is formed by a group of parents, often in the same community or neighborhood, who agree to babysit for one another. There is no charge; in fact, it's free with the agreement that you, in turn, will babysit for someone's children when the need arises. You are part of a babysitting pool and sometimes have a large list of parents to call upon when the need arises.

Like anything else, babysitting co-ops have their pros and cons. On one hand, the co-op can be great because you have a working list of 10 or more people that you know who are willing to babysit. But on the other hand, it could be a problem if you don't feel comfortable with some of the parents on the list. Another consideration is that you will be called to reciprocate when your name comes up.

Who's Watching the Kids—The ABC's of Background Checks

This is a touchy subject for many because of privacy and trust issues. It's also an uncomfortable subject because while most would agree that you should know everything about the person caring for your children, many feel uneasy about actually doing something about it.

Why be so vigilant? For the simple reason that this person will be caring for and spending considerable time alone with your most precious possessions—your children. The idea of doing a background check on someone may make you uncomfortable and that's quite normal. It is better to find out ahead of time about someone's past then to learn later on that he or she has a criminal record, has been caught driving while intoxicated, has financial problems, or tragically, is a sexual offender. You need only to watch the news to realize that children are harmed by adults they trust every day.

What if all the references you were given by the nanny or sitter check out? You should still do a background check even if his or her references are stellar. Sometimes people give an individual a glowing reference just because they would like to get rid of them. Consider that you are calling upon a stranger to tell you about another stranger that may live in your home. It's better to be vigilant and err on the side of safety than to find out that someone is not what you believed he or she to be.

What if you are hiring someone through an agency and they say that the nanny or housekeeper checked out? From time to time, an agency is not as honest as it should be. In addition, even the best, most ethical agency can make a mistake. You would be wise to verify that a background check was completed with the company that conducted the investigation.

There are two ways to investigate a person's background—either you can hire a private agency or you can attempt it on your own. A private agency will do an investigation for a fee. The turn-around time is often quick—anywhere from one to seven days. You can find a listing of investigation agencies in your local telephone directory or through the Internet. The average cost of a background check by a private agency should be around $75 to $300, depending on the depth of the investigation. A listing of several agencies found on the Web can be located in Appendix D. The following is a listing of the key areas to investigate when conducting a background search:

- **Motor Vehicle Records**—Lists all infractions in the past three to five years; confirms the status and classification of a driver's license.
- **Criminal History**—A criminal search can be done on a county, state, or federal level. The report identifies any misdemeanor or felony records, including prison parole and release records, as well as sexual offenses and convictions.
- **Social Security Number Verification**—A verification will confirm or deny if an SSN is valid. A trace on an SSN discloses the name and age of the cardholder, current and past addresses, whether the person is alive or deceased, and where the card was issued.
- **Credit History**—A credit report will reveal if he or she has ever declared bankruptcy, is in debt, or has any liens or judgments against them.

- **Worker's Compensation Reports**—Reveals any past compensation claims.

- **Previous Employer Verification**—Indicates where the person has worked, positions held, salaries, reasons for leaving, and overall job performance.

- **Educational Verification**—This report confirms where and when an individual attended school and what degrees were awarded.

In the end, you will sleep better at night knowing that you have thoroughly conducted a background search on the person caring for your children. While others may roll their eyes and say that you're going too far, remember that it is very difficult to undo a problem once it has happened.

Coming Face-to-Face

The interview process with a potential nanny or babysitter usually begins with a phone call. If the conversation goes well, then by all means, set up a face-to-face interview. Invite the best candidates to your home, one at a time, where you can observe their overall appearance, demeanor, and interaction with your children.

In meeting a candidate for the first time, ask yourself these questions:

- Did he or she arrive on time?
- Did you like his or her appearance and demeanor?
- Does the person make good eye contact with you or does he or she seem shy and withdrawn?
- How does this candidate interact with your children?
- Can you understand this person when he or she speaks?

When you meet a candidate, go over the job requirements, his or her hours, salary, and any other expectations you have for this position. This would also be the right time to find out if he or she smokes. Try to get a sense of how comfortable he or she feels in your home. Sometimes a candidate will be very agreeable over the telephone because they need the job. For example, a candidate might say that pets are not a problem, when in reality they're a big one. A few years ago, Kathy was interviewing a young woman as a housekeeper for a few hours each week. The young woman stated on the telephone that she liked pets, especially dogs. At the time, Kathy and her husband had two tremendous English Mastiffs. The young woman lasted in the house about five minutes before she began to panic and literally ran out the front door. She was so frightened that she never even closed the door behind her.

The following are some important face-to-face interview questions. Meeting a candidate is the best way to know if this is a relationship that can really work. When you ask a question, give the person the time to speak and express him or herself.

The Top 10 Questions to Ask a Potential Nanny, Au Pair, or Babysitter

1. What do you like most about children and conversely, what would you say children like the most about you?
2. What kind of experience do you have in working with children?
3. What is your idea of a difficult child and give me some examples of how you would handle that child.
4. Give me some examples of your discipline style.
5. What would be some of the activities you might do with an infant, toddler, or older child?
6. Have you ever had to call 911, and if so, what were the circumstances?
7. Do you have CPR and first aid training? Would you agree to take these courses?
8. What was your last job like and why did you leave?
9. What kinds of things do you enjoy doing when you're not working?
10. Ask the person if he or she minds if you conduct a background search. Be suspicious if he or she balks at the idea.

In the end, it may be your intuitive sense that helps make the decision about a nanny, an au pair, babysitter, or housekeeper. Eliminate any candidate from your list that makes you feel uncomfortable or pressured.

Once you have made your choice, invite the person back for an orientation at your home. This is also another good opportunity for them to get to know the children before he or she begins to work for you. Take this time to walk through the house, discuss routines, meet the pets, and go over important emergency contact numbers. If he or she is going to take the kids to school then this is the time for a driving tour of your community.

Crib Sheets

When someone comes into your home to care for the children, it's a good idea to clearly post a list of important telephone numbers in the event of an emergency.

- Where you will be: _____
- Closest friend or relative: _____
- Cell phone number: _____
- Emergency: _____
- Poison control: _____
- Police: _____
- Fire department: _____
- Hospital: _____
- Doctor: _____
- Dentist: _____
- Veterinarian: _____
- School: _____
- Dad's work number: _____
- Dad's beeper: _____
- Mom's work number: _____
- Mom's beeper: _____

Special Instructions
- Allergies: _____
- Bedtimes: _____
- Off-limits TV shows: _____
- Snacks: _____
- Approved videos _____
- Medical Consent* _____

*You might also consider having an emergency medical consent form available at your pediatrician's office. In the case of an emergency, the doctor would be able to fax the consent form to the hospital or medical center and your child would receive any emergency treatment needed.

Making Your Best Choice

Finding the right child care situation is an important part of the home office pie. Consider your children's best interests and the type of work you do when considering the kind of child care you need. Forget about trying to be bionic because there simply is no such thing. Households are busy, sometimes chaotic, noisy places with active kids, ringing phones, conflicting schedules, and barking dogs (at least in our houses). Instead of banging your head and trying to handle everything, get the help when you need it. Tap into your community and find out what others are doing and what is available to you. Your family will be better off and so will your work.

CHAPTER **13**

Strategies for Hanging in When the Going Gets Tough

It is our fervent hope and wish that everyone who buys this book in the hopes of starting a home-based business succeeds beyond their wildest expectations. Whether your dream is to make $12,000 a year and hang out with your kids while covering grocery bills and "mad money" for a yearly vacation, or your dream is to create a start-up you can eventually take public with an IPO, we hope you reach your goals.

The realists in us know that isn't going to happen for everyone. Even if you do achieve all your goals, there will be times when the "going gets tough." And just like your mom or dad used to preach to you, it's true . . . the tough get going. Even telecommuters may find times when the home office dream just is not as rosy as he or she pictured. Much of the advice in this chapter is geared toward those who form a home-based business of some sort. However, even teleworkers will gain some strategies for dealing with difficult times when you only have yourself to lean on.

Pep-Talking Yourself When You Only Hear an Echo

Everyone faces it. That day when nothing goes right. That week when nothing goes right. We've both had *years* when nothing seemed to go right. And we're not kidding.

When you work in an office with coworkers around, you can walk into the next office or cubicle and gripe. You might toss a few martinis back at happy hour and commiserate. Better yet, you might be each other's support and cheering section. But what do you do when the only voice you hear is your own?

Here are some surefire ways to get and stay motivated in the home office, especially when those tough times come calling:

- Create an off-site support system. We're not suggesting that you spend all day on the telephone crying in your cups to your best friend, but most of us do have support out there. The hardest part is *asking* for support. Rather than wait until you feel really desperate over a weak month of sales or a client who just dropped you, figure out where you're going to turn for positive support before you even make the move into the home office, and reach out via e-mail or phone, or a breakfast meeting, when you need a pick-me-up, and do the same in return.

- If you feel inspired by motivational speakers, invest in some tapes/CDs or borrow them from the library. We don't feel we have to recommend any names—you know all the biggies and plenty of rising stars below them. The point is more that the speaker should speak to *you*. Some people swear by motivational resources, and some can't stand them. If you are one who likes tapes and CDs, you may even consider having a motivational "home page" when you boot up on the Internet. Plenty of them out there will start you off each day with a compelling quote like this one from Ralph Waldo Emerson: "What lies behind us and what lies before us are tiny matters compared to what lies within us."

- Find out about people who overcame great odds and succeeded. If you're an avid reader, biographies and autobiographies by and about people like Lance Armstrong, Abraham Lincoln, Amelia Earhardt, Gloria Steinham, Martin Luther King, Jr., and business successes like Bill Gates should get you fired up.

- Break down all problems into manageable parts. Whether facing a cash crunch or a "difficult" client, try to face each problem as an individual one and not compound it all into one great big heaping pile of manure. (We wanted to use another word but our editor wouldn't let us.)

- Set goals you can complete and feel good about each day. Few people starting out selling life insurance, for example, are going to sell 5 million dollars in policies their first day. Few pharmaceutical representatives are going to penetrate the "white wall" of nurses and support staff that may stand between them and breaking open a new account first day out of the gate. Sure, it happens. But set some reasonable goals for yourself so each day you feel a sense of accomplishment. For example, don't say, "I will land five new accounts," but "I will contact five new people and land one account."

- In light of the previous point, spend some time assessing what makes you tick. Do you like To-Do lists so you can get that thrill of crossing things off it? (We admit we're both addicted to this!) Do you seem to thrive on setting very high goals for yourself? Do you find you seem to deliberately leave things to the last minute so you can work under pressure? If you really want to learn what motivates you, plug in "personality tests" on a search engine. Our search on Netscape revealed 45,000+ entries. Visiting sites showed tests to determine everything from the best career for you to how to motivate yourself. Most of the tests were free, though some companies sell them as human resources tools. In any case, if motivating yourself is something you're interested in, these tests just might tell you more about your strengths and weaknesses.

- If you find your personality (from a test or you just know this about yourself) isn't well-suited to spending huge chunks of time alone, join the Chamber of Commerce or other organizations so you get out from time to time with peers (and it's a good networking opportunity too). Many careers offer organizations from writer's guilds to accounting associations. If you live near a major city and went to a university or college with active alumni associations throughout the country, you can go to events with alumni who are usually only too happy to network with people from their old "stomping grounds."

- Use imagery to focus on what you hope to accomplish. Positive imagery is a technique used by people on sports teams like the Chicago Bulls and LA Lakers to top sales reps and motivational speakers. If it works for them, visualizing success may work for you, too. If you use imagery or its cousin, written affirmations, remember to frame things in the present tense or to use imagery that isn't about what you *might* do but what you *are doing*. For example, "I have more than enough time and energy to make my sales quota today," not "I would like to have enough time . . ." If you want to learn more about these techniques, pop in "positive thinking" on an Internet search and go crazy. Similar to buying CDs and tapes of motivational speakers, some of the books/tapes/seminars/CDs on imagery and affirmations will speak to you, and some will not. The choice is deeply personal and will likely be based on your spiritual beliefs, as well as beliefs about the power of positive thinking.

- Remember, always, why you decided to work from home. Was it to find a bit of quality time with your family? To cut down on a grueling commute? To create a business of your own? Whatever the reason, tape it to your forehead, put it on a Post-it®. Remember it on those days when the work at home routine has got you down.

- Always remember: Even on your worst day, you only had to commute 60 seconds. Turn on the TV at rush hour and watch all those cars lined up in a traffic jam as the anchors flip over to the traffic report. Listen to the traffic reporters on the radio. You walked down the hall. Case closed.

Ten Things to Do When Hard Times Happen

Everyone, eventually, faces a time when their home-based business is in danger of failing. Here are 10 things to do when a cash crunch hits or things look bleak:

1. Work your Rolodex. Then work it again. Call everyone you know and let them know how available you are for work. Erica freelances as a writer and editor. At the first sign of the slightest lull, she works the phones and let's EVERY client know she is "available" to take on a project. By the end of the day, she usually has three offers—minimum.

2. Let your accounts payable know you have a cash crunch. Offer a small discount for paying early.

3. Go outside your comfort zone. Call a friend of a friend of a friend about your business. Go to a networking happy hour even if you don't know anyone else and force yourself to talk to five people. Don't leave until you do. Comfort zones can keep you trapped.

4. Think diversification. Are you a PR writer specializing in brochures? Can you write radio commercials for a local station, too? Can you translate your skill in one area (writing and designing PR materials) to a second area (writing radio commercials)? You make desserts? Can you also teach a cooking class for both exposure to new clients and as a source of income?

5. Be persistent. Someone may have said no last month, but catch the right person on the right day and a no may turn into a yes.

6. Sell your receivables if you have a business that uses them. A 6 or 8 percent factoring charge may not be pleasant, but if you need the cash, you need the cash. Basically, this means a factoring company will advance you the money you have in receivables less 8 percent. When the money comes in, you have to sign over your checks to them.

7. Raise your prices. Sure, most people starting a business think they have to lowball to compete. They may find they've lowballed themselves into a cash-poor situation. You're worth it. Believe it. Charge it. Practice asking for it until you get comfortable. Face yourself in the mirror and say, "My fee is $1 million!" (Think big!) Then go after some new clients, and believe it or not, some people feel by paying more they're getting "the best." Have you ever bypassed a $14 polo shirt for a $30 one because you assumed the more expensive one was better? Granted, you may have felt the material and realized the quality was for the more expensive product, but the *instinct* that drove you to look at the more expensive one also drives your customer.

8. Sell more product (or services). Maybe in the past you never thought of tying two products or services together, but can you? Can you offer a deal where the customer gets a brochure done at a certain price if the customer *also* buys your press kit writing package? Maybe they called for the brochure only. Sell them more. Make it seem like a great "deal."

9. Get lean. Do you *need* the laptop you actually only use to watch movies on your business plane trips? Do you *need* to have a car and driver take you to the airport or can you park in long-term parking and save money. In tough times, big companies cut down on chauffeured limousines, parties, and perks. Do the same, even if your "perks" are considerably less grand.

10. Economize on travel and entertainment (if applicable). With teleconferencing, trips aren't as important as they used to be. And with all the extra security at airports, it's not as pleasant either (not that it ever was all that pleasant). Challenge yourself about expenses of eating out and travel. If you must travel, check out *www.expedia.com* and other Internet services that find rock-bottom bookings.

Remember These Guys?

Remember earlier on when we told you that Bill Gates, Hewlett-Packard, and others started small with big dreams? Remember that many millionaires have at one time or another had to declare personal bankruptcy (remember Donald Trump's problems?). Why? Because they're risk-takers. And risk can bring great rewards or great setbacks. So remember these risk-takers the next time you're feeling blue.

- Donald Trump
- Bill Gates
- Howard Hughes (OK, he ended up lonely and insane, but before *that* he was rich beyond his wildest imagination)
- Kate Spade
- Vera Wang
- Martha Stewart
- Francis Ford Coppolla
- Jimmy Carter (you don't think it's risky to go from peanut farmer to the White House?)

No matter what you aspire to do, there's a role model for you. So when the going gets tough . . . keep on going!

CHAPTER 14

Telecommuting Proposals: Getting into the Home Office

Many companies today—especially large ones—offer formal telecommuting or telework programs. Though some companies may prefer one term over the other, this amounts to letting someone work from home all or part of the time. However, the decision of who gets to work from home and who doesn't is often left up to individual managers. How do you get your boss to let you do that 60-second commute?

Getting Your Boss to Let You Do the 60-Second Slide to the Office

Usually, at most companies, a telecommuting proposal is the first step. If you're a trailblazer and no one at your company has telecommuted before, it's even more important that your proposal have all the i's dotted and t's crossed. Here are some guidelines:

- Demonstrate that you have thought through all the elements of telecommuting. For example, are you equipped technologically to handle the switch over to telework? Are you planning on coming in to the office for key meetings? Are all aspects of your job able to convert to being done from home?

- Anticipate arguments and create win-win responses and points within your proposal.

- Note that no formal telecommuting policy will allow you to work from home as a *replacement* for childcare. If you plan on watching your infant yourself, this will not go over well if that's somehow discovered or slips out. Most telecommuters we know have plans in place for childcare. However, if your manager is wavering just be certain that you strongly reiterate your commitment to professionalism and your job, or even let your manager know outright you have all your childcare needs handled so you will have no interruptions during your teleworking hours.

- Discuss your personality traits that make you an effective and ideal telecommuter: self-starter, flexible, independent, a good communicator, able to make workflow adjustments and adapt to crises.

- Don't resort to "whining" or complaining that "another manager lets his or her employees telework." A "no" for right now may turn into a "yes" later.

- If your manager is extremely reluctant and you are a "trailblazer," hunt the Internet and professional journals and magazines for statistics and case examples of ways in which telework is used successfully.

- Remember that some middle managers respond best to spreadsheets that give clear goals on productivity, workflow, and so forth. If facts and figures can support your case, use them.

- Try to show your productivity will actually increase without office distractions or a lengthy commute.

Flex Your Flexibility

Does telecommuting cost the worker out of pocket? It all depends on the company. Some companies will provide the telecommuter with reimbursement for office chairs, desk, laptops, networks, and dedicated lines. With this arrangement comes the spoken or unspoken agreement that no one else in the household will utilize the equipment. The laptop isn't to be used by a spouse, children, or anyone else.

At the other end of the spectrum are companies that expect the telecommuter to make the commitment to bring the home office up to speed. Erica telecommuted for three months at a publishing house. The only support she got was a disk loaded with the company's networking set-up so she could access e-mail from home. No desk, no chair, no computer. Ergonomic gel pads? Get real! It was all up to her. However, she was grateful to be able to work from home because of an asthmatic child, and she showed her flexibility by getting her home office up to speed in two days, and then launching in full steam ahead.

Regardless of what scenario your company has, it's likely a policy. If you are a trailblazer, you may need to flex your flexibility to pave the way as a teleworker and show the company it's a viable option.

We recently advised a woman on her telework proposal. Though the company in question had provided a teleworker in another department with a laptop, the verbiage of this employee's proposal included: "Though employees in X department are provided laptops for telework, should the company decline to do so in my case, I already have a PC with all the software necessary to do my job, including . . . "

This employee showed her company that she was willing to work with them either way. It all depends on how important the telecommuting opportunity is to you.

Beware of Backlash

Prejudices about the home office still linger. Nowhere is this more visible than in teleworking situations where one employee may be allowed to work from home and someone two cubicles over is not given the same privilege or opportunity. Backlash and resentment can rear their ugly heads.

To avoid this, use some common sense and courtesy, and a little extra energy:

- Be readily available. Your coworker in the next cubicle is less likely to seethe that you must be working on your golf swing and not at your desk if you are fully attentive and available. Answer the phone promptly. Have your professional voice mail. Answer e-mails as quickly and efficiently—or more so—than if you were in the office.

- Until everyone gets used to the idea, if you are a trailblazer, be extra conscientious. Post your telework hours in a prominent spot in your cubicle or office so that people don't leave interoffice mail or something needing your signature immediately and don't realize you're at home and it would be more efficient to route to someone else first.

- Deliver what you promise. If you said working from home would make you more efficient, strive to be so. Turn in projects early.

- Don't complain about the home office being lonely or boring. Sure it is sometimes. But the worker in the next department who desperately wants to be home to cut down on his commute and was denied a telework opportunity isn't going to appreciate hearing about your "woes."

- Don't brag either. While you should strive to be positive about the advantages of teleworking, don't stand around and rave about how *wonderful* it is to avoid rush hour and to be able to hug your kids or hit the tennis court right at five.

Overdoing It

In light of the common backlash that can occur when an employee makes a move to teleworking, there can be a tendency for teleworkers to overdo it. They feel they have to overcompensate for being "allowed" to work from home.

While efficiency and all the aforementioned commonsense advice is the mark of a smart telecommuter, you don't have to pull an 80-hour workweek and heap extra on your proverbial work plate to prove that you are, indeed, really working and not visiting your local tanning salon.

Let go of the guilty emotions. Step away from your desk. We're ordering you to. These are very common emotions. Said one telecommuter: "I know I do the work of two people to prove that I deserve to work from home and that I really AM working! I can't seem to let go of this workaholic tendency."

One effective way to combat this and also to prove to your superiors and peers that teleworking is a viable strategy is to track your productivity. While this can be a little tricky, sometimes it's possible. For instance, in publishing, each editor is expected to handle a certain number of "titles." When Erica teleworked, she handled an average of four more books at any one time than anyone in the office. At that point, she started to see that some of her fears that she would be perceived as "slacking" were unfounded. Which was not to say she still didn't catch the occasional dirty look.

Step back and see the big picture. After you get used to teleworking, re-mind yourself that you don't have to "prove" yourself as a worker just because you happen to work from home. Remember, as we pointed out elsewhere in the book, time that is wasted at on-site offices in useless meetings, water cooler chats, gossip, and just "downtime" is essential to sanity! You can stop and have lunch at home. You can greet your kids when they get off the school-bus before they settle in with their homework. You can have an "off" day when you have a head cold. Relax and learn to love the 60-second commute!

CHAPTER 15

MARKETING YOURSELF AND YOUR SMALL BUSINESS

W hether you are a telecommuter who needs to stay aware of the "game" and keep current with your contacts, a sales rep who needs to work your network of contacts, or a small business owner who needs to get it off the ground and keep it there, you'll likely need to market either yourself or your small business. Here are some pointers to keep in mind.

Networking is the Name of the Game

We all tend to use the term networking, but what does it really mean? How do you do it effectively?

First of all, in the dictionary sense, networking means an association of individuals with common interests who utilize that interest and group for mutual support. Chances are, we all feel we know the gist of that. But how do you network effectively? Follow these networking guidelines for the greatest chance of success.

1. Know that you are always "on." While it may not be comforting to think that you schlepped to the grocery store with a sore throat and runny nose in sweat pants and a T-shirt to pick up cold medicine and *might* run into a contact, in Murphy's Law of networking, trust us, it'll happen. The *one* time you look like a wreck will be the time you are spotted by that acquaintance who expressed interest in hearing more about your product or service. While we joke that we work in our pajamas—and sometimes do—when we go out we try to present a professional image all the time. You never know, and when you least expect it . . .

2. Use as many opportunities as possible for networking. Remember this is for "mutual support." The idea of networking isn't all *taking* and no *giving.* You might run into someone who has precisely the

computer expertise to match one of your client's needs. Vice versa, you might shake the hand of the father standing next to you at a softball game and discover he's desperately in need of a website designer for his orthodontist office—a service you are expert to provide. If you think of networking as a giant game of six degrees of separation, you won't miss an opportunity.

3. Make the call. Someone hands you a business card at a breakfast meeting of a Chamber of Commerce and says, "That's very interesting. Give me a call sometime and we'll do lunch." Make the call. Don't shove that card in your back pocket and think. "Boring guy, I'll never get any business out of him." Every person you meet knows, exponentially, many more people. For networking to be effective, you must have follow-through. If someone gives you his or her card, at least pop him or her an e-mail or a quick phone call to say, "I really appreciate your taking the time to talk to me. It was very nice meeting you, and I look forward to seeing you again." Or something along those lines.

4. Never undervalue a personal gesture. What is a personal gesture? In this age of technology, when was the last time you received a sincere, handwritten personal note? You probably have to think back. When was the last time you sent one? Another personal gesture might be that if you discussed a certain restaurant, film, business leader, and so forth and you come across an article on that topic of conversation, you might clip it or send an e-mail link to the person saying, "I thought this might be of interest to you." This technique works because everyone wants to feel as if someone in this crazy, chaotic, speeded up, technological world stopped to make a personal connection.

5. Don't forget the giving. Networking requires you to be alert for opportunities for others as well. Make a phone call to let a certain home office entrepreneur know that the chairman of a local company needs an event party-planned, and even if the party planner doesn't get the gig, he or she will remember that you tried.

6. Don't forget to listen. Ever go to a networking event and get stuck talking to someone who actually never stops for a breath and only talks about his or her business or area of expertise? Not a pleasant experience. In all social and networking interactions, don't forget

to listen. When Erica worked as a journalist, she was constantly amazed how just a simple question or two could turn into an entire feature article. Why? Because most people like talking about themselves, and many have to curb the tendency to overdo it. Ask interesting questions of people and be amazed at the results. It works.

7. If a network contact passes you along to someone else, always remember to thank him or her for that contact.

8. Remember to ask. Networking events sometimes fail because people end up gabbing at a happy hour and talking to someone and literally *forget to ask* if they can follow up with a call or forget to ask if the person might know anyone who might need his or her product or service. Same with a satisfactory job. If someone raves about the proofreading job you did, ask that person if they can recommend you to others. Sometimes people just don't think of it unless you ask— yet they're only too happy to do it.

9. The worst that can happen is they say no. That's it. A little rejection. That's the worst that can happen for asking, as in number eight. Don't take it personally. Don't brood. Don't fall apart. No. Two little letters. Get over it.

10. Go outside your comfort zone. Join organizations. Extend yourself. Shy? If you have to, work with a free SCORE business counselor to work on strategies. But the bottom line is that most successful people don't have success land in their laps. They have to go outside their comfort zone. They have to cold call. They have to go speak to that client who yelled at them over a late delivery. Sincerity goes a long way with that, by the way. Move outside your comfort zone. Force yourself. Say, "I will not get off the phones today until I make 10 cold calls." Cognitive behavioral therapy will tell you the more you do something, the easier it gets to do it!

PR Tips

The tough thing about writing a book about the 60-second commute is the broad range of businesses and services and telecommuting opportunities that are limited only by readers' imaginations: We can't tell you PR and marketing strategies for each. So here are a few general tools and tips to apply to almost any business.

- Revisit Chapter Six, on professionalism. Regardless of your business, put your most professional foot forward in terms of brochures, websites, and business cards.

- Think outside the box. Sure, you may have started your business on your kitchen table. Maybe you're a typist and word processor. Maybe a PR writer. Maybe you make homemade desserts. Can you donate some of your services to a worthy cause? Can you tie your business into an event happening in the media or in your community? For example, Erica's daughter is in a youth symphony and every year they hold a black tie event. Someone with a homemade dessert business just may find himself or herself swamped after providing delectables for free after just one high-profile event.

- Join the Chamber of Commerce, Rotary Club, and other organizations, such as alumni chapters of your college if you attended college. These opportunities for networking may also present you with marketing opportunities. For instance, often joining the Chamber of Commerce (for a fee) will give you a "free" ad in their glossy chamber magazine or at least a phone listing.

- Payback time. Have you gone to the same hair salon for 10 years? Do you go to the same OB-GYN or family practice doctor that you went to since you became an adult? Do you frequent the same small boutique or bakery week after week. Well, it's payback time. There's no harm in asking whether you can leave your business cards on the counter or in a visible spot. Don't be shy! And think of cross-connections. Real-life example? All the nurses in Erica's OB-GYN office wore beautiful angel pins. And there on the counter was a business card holder with the jewelry maker's cards. Mothers feel like new life symbolizes angels. The jewelry maker was a patient. Voilà. Every woman paying her co-insurance fee stood at that counter, saw those pins on the nurses, and I bet many of them took a card. Note this is "free" marketing. You don't have to advertise on cable TV or in a newspaper to get the word out.

- Work that Rolodex and Yellow Pages. Can your business be used at a local college or university (e.g., typing services)? What about churches? Temples? Senior citizens housing? Cast a wide net about who can use your business or service and then think of how to reach those people. Call the director of a new big company in town that will be having lots of people relocated to its offices. Let them know you have a home day care and plenty of terrific references. Let a hospital know you hire out as a clown. Let a new charter school know you design brochures. Scan your local newspaper for new businesses and events, and then call them! Don't wait for word of mouth, though that's important. Be proactive.

The Success Monster

Sure, we've seen the statistics. Many home businesses fail. But what about the triumphant successes? If you follow all these marketing strategies, you just may find yourself in a position where you are "too successful." Actually, there's no such thing. But we thought this would be a good point to add a caveat that if you find yourself working 24/7, for a sustained period with no sign of let-up, it might be time to add a support person or assistant to your home office.

Success can literally be destructive. Erica knows firsthand. She got so busy she didn't have "time" to file, do her taxes properly, or even eat on some days. It's a nice problem to confront, but it is still a problem. Know when you're hitting burnout. Are you short-tempered, never getting enough sleep, never taking a lunch break? It may be time to take a hard look at how successful you've become and look at how you can add some balance in your life, perhaps by hiring an employee or two. It's a scary step . . . but someday you'll look back and see it as a turning point.

APPENDIX A

GOVERNMENT RESOURCES

There is a wealth of government agencies to contact that can provide you with free information and expert advice to guide you with any particular questions you may have.

- **Better Business Bureau,** 4200 Wilson Blvd., Suite 800, Arlington, VA 22203-1838, (703) 276-0100, fax: (703) 525-8277, *www.bbb.org*

- **Canadian Council of the Better Business Bureau,** 44 Byward Market Square, Suite 220, Ottawa, Ontario K1N 7A2, e-mail: ccbbb@canadiancouncilbbb.ca

- **Consumer Information Center (CIC),** P.O. Box 100, Pueblo, CO 81002, (800) FED-INFO, *www.pueblo.gsa.gov*

- **Consumer Product Safety Commission (CPSC),** Publications Request, Washington, DC 20207, (301) 504-0990, fax: (302) 504-0124, e-mail: info@cpsc.gov, *www.cpsc.gov*

- **Copyright Office,** Library of Congress, 101 Independence Ave., SE, Washington, DC 20559-6000, (202) 707-3000, *www.lcweb.loc.gov/copyright/*

- **Federal Trade Commission (FTC),** Consumer Response Center, Federal Trade Commission—CRC-240, Washington, DC 20580, (202) 326-2000 or (202) 236-2222, or (877) FTC-HELP, *www.ftc.gov*

- **Immigration and Naturalization Service.** For a local field office in your area, call (800) 870-3676 or visit *www.ins.usdoj.gov*

- **National Consumers League,** 1701 K St., NW, Suite 1200, Washington, DC 20006, (202) 835-3323, e-mail: info@nclnet.org

- **National Fraud Information Center,** P.O. Box 65868, Washington, DC 20035, (800) 876-7060, *www.fraud.org*

- **National Women's Business Council,** 409 Third St., SW, Suite 210, Washington, DC 20004, (202) 205-3850, fax: (202) 205-6825

- **Office of Small and Disadvantaged Business Utilization (OSDBU),** 14th and Constitution Ave., NW, HCHB Room 6411, Washington, DC 20230, (202) 482-1472, fax: (202) 482-0501, e-mail: NFenner1@doc.gov

- **Small Business Administration (SBA),** 409 Third St., SW, Washington, DC 20416, (800) 827-5722, *www.sbaonline.sba.gov/ starting/indexsteps.html*

- **Superintendent of Documents,** Government Printing Office, Washington, DC 20402, *www.access.gpo.gov*

- **U.S. Bureau of Census,** Customer Service, Washington, DC 20233, (301) 457-4100, *www.census.gov*

- **U.S. Department of Agriculture (USDA),** 12th St. and Independence Ave., SW, Washington, DC 20250

- **U.S. Department of Commerce (DOC),** Office of Business Liaison, 14th St. and Constitution Ave., NW, Room 5898C, Washington, DC 20230, *www.doc.gov*

- **U.S. Department of Labor (DOL),** Employment Standards Administration, 200 Constitution Ave., NW, Washington, DC 20210, *www.dol.gov*

- **U.S. Department of Treasury, The Internal Revenue Service (IRS),** P.O. Box 25866, Richmond, VA 23260, (800) 424-3676, *www.irs.gov*

- **U.S. Environmental Protection Agency (EPA),** Small Business Ombudsman, 401 M St., SW, (A-149C), Washington, DC 20460, (703) 557-1938, all others: (800) 368-5888

- **U.S. Food and Drug Administration (FDA), FDA Center for Food Safety and Applied Nutrition,** 200 Charles St., NW, Washington, DC 20402, *www.fda.gov*

- **U.S. Patent and Trademark Office,** Crystal Plaza 3, Room 2CO2, Washington, DC 20231, (800) 786-9199, *www.uspto.gov*

- **U.S. Securities and Exchange Commission,** 450 Fifth St., NW, Washington, DC 20549, (202) 942-7040, e-mail: help@sec.gov, *www.sec.gov*

APPENDIX B

ORGANIZATIONS AND ASSOCIATIONS

Organizations and associations are wonderful places to turn for information, advice, and meeting others who share your interests. Many provide workshops, offer seminars, and publish newsletters. They are also a surefire way to network and learn about potential opportunities in your field.

- **Alliance of Claims Assistance Professionals,** 731 South Naperville Rd., Wheaton, IL 60187, (630) 588-1260, *www.claims.org*
- **American Association of Franchises and Dealers,** P.O. Box 81887, San Diego, CA 92138-1887, (800) 733-9858, fax: (619) 209-3777, *www.aafd.org*
- **American Association of Home-Based Businesses,** P.O. Box 10023, Rockville, MD 20849, (800) 447-9710, fax: (301) 963-7042, e-mail: aahbb@crosslink.net, *www.aahbb.org*
- **American Association of Medical Transcriptionists,** P.O. Box 576187, Modesto, CA 95357, (209) 551-0883, fax: (209) 551-9317, *www.aamt.org*
- **American Business Women's Association,** 9100 Ward Parkway, P.O. Box 8728, Kansas City, MO 64114-0728, (816) 361-6621, fax: (816) 361-4991, e-mail: abwa@abwahq.org
- **American Council of Nanny Schools,** Delta College, Room A-67, University Center, MI 48710, (517) 686-9417
- **American Franchisee Association (AFA),** 53 West Jackson Blvd., Suite 205, Chicago, IL 60603, (800) 334-4232, fax: (312) 431-1132, *www.franchisee.org/*
- **American Institute of Certified Public Accountants,** 1211 Avenue of the Americas, 6th Floor North, New York, NY 10036, (212) 596-6200, fax: (212) 596-6213, *www.aicpa.org*

- **American Intellectual Property Law Association,** 2001 Jefferson Davis Highway, Suite 203, Arlington, VA 22202, (703) 415-0780, fax: (703) 415-0786, *www.aipla.org*
- **American Home Business Association, Inc.,** 4505 South Wasatch Blvd., Suite 140, Salt Lake City, UT, 84124, (800) 556-9150, *www.homebusiness.com*
- **American Marketing Association,** 311 S. Wacker Dr., Suite 5800, Chicago, IL 60606, (800) AMA-1150, (312) 542-9000, fax: (312) 542-9001, e-mail: info@ama.org, *www.ama.org*
- **American Screenwriters Association,** P.O. Box 12860, Cincinnati, OH 45212, (513) 731-9212, *www.asascreenwriters.com*
- **American Society of Inventors,** P.O. Box 58426, Philadelphia, PA 19102, (215) 546-6601, *www.americaninventor.org*
- **American Society of Journalists and Authors,** 1501 Broadway, Suite 302, New York, NY, (212) 997-0947, fax: (212) 758-7414, *www.asja.org*
- **American Telecommuting Association,** 1220 L Street, NW, Suite 100, Washington, DC 20005, (800) ATA-4-YOU, *www.knowledgetree.com/ata.html*
- **American Woman's Economic Development Corp.,** 216 E. 45th Street, 10th Floor, New York, NY 10017, (212) 692-9100, fax: (212) 692-9296
- **Asian Women in Business (AWIB),** 1 W. 34th St., Suite 200, New York, NY 10001, (212) 868-1368, e-mail: info@awib.org
- **Association of On-Line Professionals,** 6096 Franconia Rd., Suite D, Alexandria, VA 22310, (703) 924-5800, fax: (703) 924-5801, *www.aop.org*
- **Association of Small Business Development Centers,** 3108 Columbia Pike, Suite 300, Arlington, VA 22204, (703) 271-8700, fax: (703) 271-8701, e-mail: info@asbdc-us.org, *www.asbdc-us.org*
- **Association of Temporary and Staffing Services,** 119 South Saint Asaph St., Alexandria, VA 22314, (703) 549-6387, *www.natss.org*
- **Au Pair in America,** River Plaza, 9 West Broad St., Stamford, CT 06902-3788, (800) 928-7247, *www.aifs.org*
- **Business Marketing Association,** 400 N. Michigan Ave., 15th Floor, Chicago, IL 60611, (800) 664-4262, fax: (312) 409-4266, *www.marketing.org*

- **Canadian Authors Association,** P.O. Box 419, Campbellford, Ontario, Canada K0L 1L0, (705) 653-0323, fax: (705) 653-0593, *www.CanAuthors.org*

- **Canadian Telework Association,** 52 Stonebriar Dr., Nepean, Ontario, Canada K2G 5X9, *www.ivc.ca*

- **Catalyst,** 120 Wall St., New York, NY 10005, (212) 514-7600, fax: (212) 514-8470, e-mail: info@catalystwomen.org

- **Center for Entrepreneurial Management Inc.,** 180 Varick St., Penthouse, New York, NY 10014, (212) 633-0060, fax: (212) 633-0063, *www.ceoclubs.org*

- **Child Care Action Campaign,** 330 7th Ave., 17th Floor, New York, NY 10001, (212) 239-0138

- **Direct Marketing Association,** 1120 Avenue of the Americas, New York, NY 10036, (212) 768-7277, fax: (212) 768-7277, *www.the-dma.org*

- **Direct Selling Association,** 1666 K St., NW, Suite 1010, Washington, DC 20006-2808, (202) 263-5760, fax: (202) 463-4569, *www.dsa.org*

- **Disnet,** 17 Sara Dr., Robbinsville, NJ 08691-2541, (609) 448-5685, fax: (609) 448-5685, e-mail: info@disnet1.org, *www.disnet1.org*

- **Editorial Freelancers Association,** 71 West 23rd St., Suite 1910, New York, NY 10010, (212) 929-5400, fax: (212) 929-5439, *www.the-efa.org*

- **EurAuPair,** 250 N. Coast Highway, Laguna Beach, CA 92651, (800) 333-3804, *www.euraupair.com*

- **Home Business Institute,** P.O. Box 301, White Plains, NY 10606-0301, (914) 946-6600, (888) 342-5424, fax: (914) 946-6694, *www.hbiweb.com*

- **Home Office Association of America,** 10 Gracie Station, P.O. Box 806, New York, NY 10028-0082, (800) 809-4622, fax: (212) 535-7240, *www.hoaa.com*

- **Independent Homeworkers Alliance,** 180 James St. South, Suite 300, Hamilton, Ontario, Canada L8P 4V1, (905) 521-9888, e-mail: info@homeworkers.org, *www.homeworkers.org*

- **International Association of Financial Planning,** 5775 Glenridge Dr., NE, Suite B-300, Atlanta, GA 30328, (404) 845-0011, *www.iafp.org*

- **LEADS,** P.O. Box 279, Carlsbad, CA 92018, (760) 434-3761, (800) 783-3761, *www.leadsclub.com*

- **Mother's Home Business Network,** P.O. Box 423, East Meadow, NY 11554, (516) 997-7394, fax: (516) 997-0839, *www.homeworkingmom.com*
- **National Association for the Education of Young Children,** 1509 16th St., NW, Washington, DC 20036, (800) 424-2460, *www.naeyc.org/naeyc*
- **National Association for Family Child Care,** 206 6th Ave., Suite 900, Des Moines, IA 50309, (515) 282-8192
- **National Association for the Self-Employed,** P.O. Box 612067, DFW Airport, Dallas, TX 75261-2067, (800) 232-6273, *www.nase.org*
- **National Association of Black Telecommunications Professionals, Inc.,** 1710 H St., NW, 10th Floor, Washington, DC 20006-4601, (800) 946-6228, *www.nabtp.org*
- **National Association of Childcare Resource and Referral Agencies,** 126 Wood Lake Dr., SE, Rochester, MN 55904, (507) 287-2020, toll free: (800) 462-1660
- **National Association of Home Based Businesses,** 10451 Mill Run Circle, Owings Mills, MD 21117, (410) 363-3698, e-mail: nahbb.msn.com, *www.usahomebusiness.com*
- **National Association of Professional Employer Organizations,** 901 North Pitt St., Suite 350, Alexandria, VA 22314, (703) 836-0466, *www.napeo.org*
- **National Association of Professional Organizers,** P.O. Box 140647, Austin, TX 78714, (512) 454-8626, fax: 512-454-3036, *www.napo.net*
- **National Association of Small Business Investment Companies,** 666 11th St., NW, Suite 750, Washington, DC 20001, (202) 628-5055, fax: (202) 628-5080, e-mail: nasbic.org, *www.nasbic.org*
- **National Association for Women Business Owners (NAWBO),** 1377 K St. NW, Suite 637, Washington, DC 20005, e-mail: national@nawbo.org
- **National Center for Employee Ownership (NCEO),** 1201 Martin Luther King Jr. Way, 2nd Floor, Oakland, CA 94612, (510) 272-9461, fax: (510) 272-9510, e-mail: nceo@nceo.org
- **National Electronic Billers Association (NEBA),** 1730 South Amphlett Blvd., Suite 217, San Mateo, CA 94402, (650) 359-4419, *www.nebazone.com*

- **National Federation of Independent Businesses,** 53 Century Blvd., Nashville, TN 37214, (800) NFIB-NOW, fax: (800) 274-6342, *www.nfib.com*

- **National Foundation for Women Business Owners (NFWBO),** 1100 Wayne Ave., Suite 830, Silver Spring, MD 20910-5603, (301) 495-4975, fax: (301) 495-4979, e-mail: NFWBO@world-net.att.net

- **National Inventors Foundation,** 403 South Central Ave., Glendale, CA 91204, (818) 246-6546, (877) IDEA-BIN, *www.inventions.org*

- **National Minority Business Council (NMBC),** 235 E. 42nd St., New York, NY 10017, (212) 573-2385, fax: (212) 573-4462, e-mail: nmbc@msn.com

- **National Small Business United,** 1156 15th St., NW, Suite 1100, Washington, DC 20005, (202) 293-8830, fax: (202) 872-8543, *www.nsbu.org*

- **National Venture Capital Association,** 1655 N. Ft. Myer Dr., Suite 850, Arlington, VA 22209, (703) 524-2549, fax: (703) 524-3940, *www.nvca.org*

- **Small Business Benefit Association,** 1112 East Range Rd., Salt Lake City, UT 84117, (801) 446-1091, fax: (801) 446-1092, *www.sbba.com*

- **Small Office Home Office Association (SOHOA),** 1767 Business Center Dr., Suite 450, Reston, VA 20190, (888) SOHOA11, *www.sohoa.com*

- **Society of Financial Service Professionals,** 270 Bryn Mawr Ave., Bryn Mawr, PA 19010, (610) 526-2500, *www.financialpro.org*

- **Telecommunications Industry Association,** 1300 Pennsylvania Ave., Suite 350, Washington, DC 20004, (202) 383-1480, fax: (202) 383-1495, *www.tiaonline.org*

- **United States Association for Small Business and Entrepreneurship,** 975 University Ave., Suite 3260, Madison, WI 53706, (608) 262-9982, fax: (608) 263-0818, *www.usasbe.org*

- **Working Today,** 55 Washington St., Suite 557, Brooklyn, NY 11201, (718) 222-1099, (866) 420-5807, fax: (718) 222-4440, (866) 420-5809, e-mail: info@workingtoday.org, *www.workingtoday.org*

APPENDIX C

START-UP ASSISTANCE

When you're at square one and just starting out with a home office, the details can feel daunting. The sites listed below are terrific because they cover everything you should know and more.

- **Small Business Administration (SBA):** This is the SBA website filled with information for start-up businesses. With versions in both English and Spanish, this site provides start-up kits, business plans, online counseling, workshops, shareware, and conference information. Visit: *www.sbaonline.sba.gov*

- **Myprimetime's Entrepreneur Toolkit:** If you're still wrestling with the idea of becoming an entrepreneur, this website is worth visiting. Visit: *www.myprimetime.com/work/entrepreneur_toolkit*

- **Business Know-How®:** This website provides information about business plans, business agreements, marketing, management, direct sales, selling hints, and much more. Visit: *www.businessknowhow.com*

- **U.S. Business Advisor:** A clearinghouse for small business information including business plans, strategies, legal issues, taxes, and government loans. Visit: *www.business.gov*

APPENDIX **D**

WEB HOT SPOTS

Like traveling through space, the Internet can seem boundless. With so many websites, it is easy to get overwhelmed by too much information. The sites listed here were chosen for their depth and variety of information regarding small businesses and telecommuters and provide clear, step-by-step advice, ideas, and overall usefulness.

Business

- About.com   *www.about.com/smallbusiness*
- American Incorporators Ltd.   *www.ailcorp.com*
- BenefitMall   *www.benefitmall.com*
- BusinessCards.com   *www.businesscards.com*
- Click & Inc.   *www.clickandinc.com*
- Company Sleuth   *www.companysleuth.com*
- eHealthInsurance.com   *www.ehealthinsurance.com*
- Entrepreneur.com   *www.entrepreneur.com*
- Federal Express   *www.fedex.com*
- Inc.com   *www.inc.com*
- Insurance Information Exchange   *www.iix.com*
- Insurance Information Institute   *www.iii.org*
- InterNic   *www.internic.net*
- MadeE-Z.com   *www.madeE-Z.com*
- Paper Direct   *www.paperdirect.com*
- Small Business Administration   *www.sba.gov*
- U.S. Business Advisor   *www.business.gov*

- Working Solo   *www.workingsolo.com*
- Zoomerang   *www.zoomerang.com*

Child Care

- Access Background Checks   *www.accesschecks.com*
- Backgrounds Online   *www.backgroundsonline.com*
- BlueSuitMom.com   *www.bluesuitmom.com*
- Everything4Nanny   *www.4nanny.com*
- Families and Work   *www.familiesandwork.org*
- Fatherhood Project   *www.fatherhoodproject.org*
- Myprimetime   *www3.myprimetime.com*
- ParentsPlace.com   *www.parentsplace.com*
- ParentSoup.com   *www.parentsoup.com*
- Practical Parenting   *www.practicalparenting.com*
- The Childcare Center.com   *www.thechildcarecenter.com*
- Working Mother   *www.workingmother.com*

Entrepreneurs

- About.com   *www.about.com/smallbusiness*
- Entrepreneur.com   *www.entrepreneur.com*
- Entrepreneurial Edge Online   *www.edgeonline.com*
- Fairmark Press   *www.fairmark.com*
- Forbes.com   *www.forbes.com*
- Fortune.com   *www.fortune.com*
- Franchising.com   *www.franchising.com*
- Idea Café   *www.ideacafe.com*
- Inc.com   *www.inc.com*
- Oracle Small Business Suite   *www.oraclesmallbusiness.com*
- American Express   *www.americanexpress.com/ smallbusiness*

Job Hunting

- Cooljob.com   *www.cooljobs.com*

- CareerBuilder.com www.careerbuilder.com
- CareerShop.com www.careershop.com
- Flip Dog www.flipdog.com
- HotJobs.com www.hotjobs.com
- Monster.com www.monster.com
- Quintessential Careers www.quintcareers.com
- WetFeet.com www.wetfeet.com

Legal

- FreeAdvice www.freeadvice.com
- LawGuru.com www.lawguru.com
- Lawyers.com www.lawyers.com
- Martindale.com www.martindale.com
- Nolo.com Law for All www.nolo.com

Taxes

- About.com www.about.com/smallbusiness
- Idea Café www.ideacafe.com
- Intuit www.qfn.com/taxcenter
- IRS Online www.ustreas.gov
- Quicken.com www.quicken.com/taxes
- TaxPlanet.com www.taxplanet.com
- Yahoo Finance Tax Center taxes.yahoo.com

Talkin' Trash: For those moments when you're feeling lonely for the gang back at the office

- Monster.com www.monster.com
- The Smoking Gun www.thesmokinggun.com
- Vault.com www.thevault.com
- WetFeet.com www.wetfeet.com

Trademark and Intellectual Properties

- U.S. Patent and Trademark Office www.uspto.gov

- U.S. Copyright Office   *www.lcweb.loc.gov/copyright*
- NameProtect.com   *www.nameprotect.com*

Women in Business

- iVillage.com   *www.ivillage.com*
- Working Woman   *www.workingwoman.com*
- Women's Work   *www.wwork.com*

GLOSSARY

Balance sheet: A balance sheet is a summary of what your business is worth (assets) versus what your company owes (liabilities). Assets include cash, accounts receivables, inventory, and equipment. Liabilities include debts to creditors, loans to banks, accounts payable, and income taxes.

Business plan: Consider a business plan as your road map for plotting out how you will manage, market, finance, plan, and set future goals for your business.

Cable Modem: This modem allows you to access the Internet through your cable line. It also requires an alteration in your computer that your cable company will install (usually called a "surfboard").

Calendar year: A type of tax year, the calendar year reflects a 12-month accounting period starting with January 1st and finishing on December 31st of each year. Most companies choose to use this form of tax year because it coincides with their personal income filing.

Cash flow statement: Analyzes the money that comes in versus the money that goes out.

COBRA: See *Consolidated Omnibus Budget Reconciliation Act* of 1985.

Color Psychology: A discipline of psychology that examines how color can affect a person's mood and energy levels.

Consolidated Omnibus Budget Reconciliation Act: Enacted in 1985, COBRA, as it is better known, provides a way for people to continue their health care insurance after they have left their jobs.

Copyright: A copyright protects your expression of an idea and prevents others from using an original work of expression such as art, music, and books without the written consent of the copyright owner.

Corporate bylaws: Created by the corporation, bylaws describe how the corporation will run. The bylaws of a corporation describe the responsibilities of the shareholders, corporate officers, and board of directors.

CPU: Stands for Central Processing Unit. It's the "guts" of your computer.

DBA: "Doing business as." Known also as a fictitious business name, a DBA indicates that you are operating a business under a name other than your own. Typically, the county and state require that the name is registered and a certificate is obtained.

DSL Lines (Digital Subscriber Lines): Digital subscriber lines are used for Internet access and transmit over copper lines, and require that you be a certain distance from a DSLAM (a type of master equipment). DSL offers lightning fast connections and excellent reliability.

e-Commerce: The business of doing business on the Internet.

Employee: According to the IRS, an individual is an employee of your business if you control what will be done, how it will be done, and what the salary will be.

Employer identification number: Also known as a EIN, an employer identification number identifies your business for tax filing purposes, much like a social security number identifies you as a taxpayer. It is issued by the IRS and appears in a nine-digit format that looks like this: 00-0000000.

Feng Shui: For practitioners, this is a way of contemplating space in a home or office and creating harmony, health, peace of mind, and wealth. Usually considered a Chinese discipline or science, there are now American schools and practitioners from all backgrounds.

FICA: Formerly known as the Federal Insurance Contributions Act, FICA is actually two taxes rolled into one (Social Security and Medicare taxes) and are withheld from your paycheck.

Fiscal year: A type of tax year, the fiscal year covers a 12-month period and refers to the accounting period used for your financial records and for filing to the IRS.

FUTA: Formerly known as the Federal Unemployment Tax Act, FUTA is paid separately from FICA and withholding income tax. FUTA taxes are paid by employers for the purpose of compensating employees who lose their jobs.

Hard Drive Memory: Different from RAM. These are the physical hard disks that actually hold the programs and the data. A computer can have more than one of them, and users can buy many gigabytes of hard disk memory for a fraction of what such internal storage capacity once cost.

Independent contractor: According to the IRS, an independent contractor is a self-employed individual who is hired to do a specific job by a company or person but who is not controlled by that company or person.

Instant Messaging: Instant messaging (IM) software allows users to "chat" in "real time" and receive messages pretty much instantly, as the name implies. For corporate needs, most IM software now includes "tracking" capabilities to follow a stream of dialogue.

Intellectual property: Intellectual properties, or IP's, refer to the unique ideas, product designs, formulas, recipes, logo, articles, or jingles that are protected under the law by a trademark, trade secret, patent, or copyright.

Internet Provider: America Online (AOL) remains the most popular provider. Others include Microsoft Outlook, Hotmail, Yahoo! and so on. The Internet provider is the "pathway" if you will or the access point onto which you can jump on and "surf" the Internet

ISDN: Integrated Services Digital Network, is a service provided by local telephone companies. By modifying regular telephone lines, ISDN allows you to transmit data significantly faster than even the fastest regular or analog modems, as well as transmit large files. ISDN lets users transmit data, voice, and video simultaneously on one line.

JAZZ drive: Similar to a Zip drive but holds almost a gigabyte of memory.

Nondisclosure agreement: Also known as confidentiality agreements or NDA's, a nondisclosure agreement is a document that protects your designs, business formulas, client lists, and trade secrets from being used by anyone else without your written consent.

Patents: A patent protects the invention and works of an inventor from being stolen or copied by somebody else.

Profit and loss statement: Also known as a P&L, a profit and loss statement shows how much money your business is bringing in and how much your business is spending.

Public domain: Anyone can use certain works in music, art, and literature because there are no copyright laws placed upon them. Federal government publications fall under public domain and can be used freely by everyone.

Quarterly taxes: Quarterly taxes are paid by self-employed individuals who do not have employer withholding income tax taken from their paychecks each week. These taxes are called quarterly taxes because they are paid on a quarterly schedule.

RAM: Random access memory.

Service mark: A trademark for service indicating that your business name is nationally registered and protected under federal law.

Stock shares: Stock shares represent a percentage of ownership in a corporation.

Tax year: A tax year refers to the accounting period used for your financial records, reporting income and expenses, and filing to the IRS. There are two types of tax years – calendar year and fiscal year.

Telecommuting: A term used to describe people who "commute" to the "on-site" office of a company from an "off-site" or satellite location. Can be used interchangeably with "Teleworking," though some individuals or companies may approve of one term over another.

Teleworking: See Telecommuting.

Term Life Insurance: Term life insurance does not have a cash surrender value. Premiums are cheaper.

Trademark: A trademark (^{TM}) is a name, symbol, catchy word or phrase, or device that makes your product easily identifiable and distinguishes it from others.

Trade secret: A trade secret can be a formula, recipe, customer list or an invention that gives you the upper hand over your competitors.

Whole Life Insurance: Whole life has a cash surrender value. Premiums are higher than term life insurance.

Zip drive: A Zip can hold about 100 megabytes of information. A Zip drive is used, most often, for backing up critical files and for transferring files from one computer to another.

REFERENCES

1. Anthony, Joseph (1995). *Working for Yourself: Full-time, Part-time, Any Time*. Washington, DC: Kiplinger Books.

2. Bangs, David, H. & Axman, Andi (1998). *Launching Your Home-Based Business: How to Successfully Plan, Finance, and Grow Your New Venture*. Chicago: Upstart Publishing.

3. Bleecker, Arlene (2001). *Getting Organized! Tips to Save You Time and Money*. Boca Raton, FL: American Media Mini Mags, Inc.

4. Cook, Mel (1998). *Home Business, Big Business*. New York: Macmillan.

5. Edwards, Paul, Edwards, Sarah, and Economy, Peter (2000). *Home-Based Business for Dummies*. New York: Hungry Minds.

6. Edwards, Paul, and Edwards, Sarah (1999). *Working From Home: Everything You Need to Know About Living and Working Under the Same Roof*. New York: Putnam.

7. Fisher, Lionel, L. (1995). *On Your Own: A Guide to Working Happily, Productively and Successfully From Home*. New Jersey: Prentice-Hall.

8. Graham, Stedman (1997). *You Can Make It Happen: A Nine-Step Plan for Success*. New York: Simon & Schuster.

9. "How Long Is the Average Work Week in the U.S.?," *www.libraryspot.com*, 3/18/02.

10. Lesonsky, Rieva (2001). *Start Your Own Business*. Irvine, CA: Entrepreneur Media, Inc.

11. Lockwood, Georgene (1999). *The Complete Idiot's Guide to Organizing Your Life*. Indianapolis, IN: Alpha Books.

12. McGeveran, William, A. (2001). *The World Almanac and Book Of Facts 2001*. Mahwah, NJ: World Book Almanac Books.

13. Morgenstern, Julie (1998). *Organizing From the Inside Out: The Foolproof System for Organizing Your Home, Your Office, and Your Life*. New York: Henry Holt and Company.

14. Morgenstern, Julie (2000). *Time Management From the Inside Out: The Foolproof System for Taking Control of Your Schedule and Your Life*. New York: Henry Holt and Company.

15. Navas, John, "Five Myths of DSL Broadband: The Truth Just Might Set You Free (from Grief).", *www.techtv.com*, February 26, 2001.

16. Norman, Jan (1999). *What No One Ever Tells You About Starting Your Own Business*. New York: Perigree Books.

17. Parlapiano, Ellen, H. and Cobe, Patricia (1996). *Mompreneurs: A Mother's Practical Step-By-Step Guide to Work-At-Home Success*. New York.

18. Peel, Kathy (1998). *The Family Manager's Everyday Survival Guide*. New York: Ballantine Books.

19. Peel, Kathy (2000). *Be Your Best: The Family Manager's Guide to Personal Success*. New York: Ballantine Books.

20. Savage, Jack (2000). *The Everything Home-Based Business Book*. Holbrook, MA: Adams Media Corporation.

21. Sheedy, Edna (1998). *Home-Based Business*. Vancouver, British Columbia: Self-Counsel Press.

22. Silvester, James, L. (1995*). How to Start, Finance, and Operate Your Own Business*. New York: Birch Lane Press.

23. Spiegel, Robert (2000). *The Complete Guide to Home Business*. New York: Amacom.

INDEX

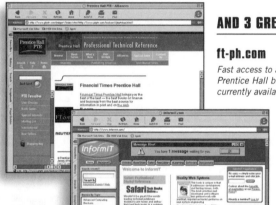

8 reasons why you should read the Financial Times for 4 weeks RISK-FREE!

To help you stay current with significant
developments in the world economy ...
and to assist you to make informed business
decisions — the Financial Times brings you:

❶ Fast, meaningful overviews of international affairs ... plus daily
briefings on major world news.

❷ Perceptive coverage of economic, business, financial and political
developments with special focus on emerging markets.

❸ More international business news than any other publication.

❹ Sophisticated financial analysis and commentary on world market
activity plus stock quotes from over 30 countries.

❺ Reports on international companies and a section on global investing.

❻ Specialized pages on management, marketing, advertising and
technological innovations from all parts of the world.

❼ Highly valued single-topic special reports (over 200 annually)
on countries, industries, investment opportunities, technology and more.

❽ The Saturday Weekend FT section — a globetrotter's guide to
leisure-time activities around the world: the arts, fine dining, travel,
sports and more.

FT FINANCIAL TIMES
World business newspaper

The *Financial Times* delivers a world of business news.

Use the Risk-Free Trial Voucher below!

To stay ahead in today's business world you need to be well-informed on a daily basis. And not just on the national level. You need a news source that closely monitors the entire world of business, and then delivers it in a concise, quick-read format.

With the *Financial Times* you get the major stories from every region of the world. Reports found nowhere else. You get business, management, politics, economics, technology and more.

Now you can try the *Financial Times* for 4 weeks, absolutely risk free. And better yet, if you wish to continue receiving the *Financial Times* you'll get great savings off the regular subscription rate. Just use the voucher below.